POLARISAT[...]
SOCIAL HO[...]

PETER WILLMOTT
and
ALAN MURIE

Policy Studies Institute

PSI Publications are obtainable from all good bookshops, or by visiting the Institute at: 100 Park Village East, London NW1 3SR (01-387 2171).

Sales Representation: Pinter Publishers Ltd.

Individual and Bookshop orders to: Marston Book Services Ltd, P.O. Box 87, Oxford, OX4 1LB.

A CIP catalogue record of this book is available from the British Library.

PSI Research Report 676

ISBN 0 85374 350 9

Printed by Bourne Offset Ltd, Iver, Bucks.

Sheffield City Polytechnic

Department of Urban & Regional Studies

Contents

Acknowledgements

The study on which this report is based was funded by the Nuffield Foundation. We had initially hoped that our French associates would secure enough funding to allow them to contribute a substantial French element to a comparative study, one which would have been as much about France as about Britain. That did not prove possible, and we have therefore had to treat French social housing in less depth than we had planned.

We were helped by an advisory panel, whose members were Michael Burbidge, Chris Hamnett, Michael Harloe, Alan Holmans, Judith Littlewood, Duncan Maclennan, Jane Morton, Chris Watson, Christine Whitehead and Peter Williams. Other British colleagues who commented on drafts were Peter Emms, Peter Malpass, Tim Melville-Ross, Murray Stewart, Phyllis Willmott and Marie Winkler.

Our main guidance on French social housing came from our associates at the Centre de Recherche sur L'Habitat - Nicole Haumont, Antoine Haumont and Henri Raymond. Other French colleagues who gave advice and help were Michel Amzallag, Anne Gotman, Jean-Michel Léger, Anne-Marie Pantaleon, Nicole Martin, Jean Rousseau and Jean-Claude Toubon.

1   Introduction

Council housing has served Britain well in the century of its existence. It provided large quantities of decent housing at reasonable rents. It weakened the link between income poverty and housing poverty, so that those whose earnings were low were not necessarily condemned to live in homes which were overcrowded or lacked running hot water, bathrooms and WCs. It was in its time a marvellous jewel in the crown of civic enterprise.

In the last decade or so the picture has changed. Council housing as a whole has become more and more the preserve of poor people. And within the council sector the poorest and most disadvantaged have more and more had to live on the worst estates. Britain is splitting into two nations: a majority living in decent houses which they own themselves and a minority condemned to the worst of the stock.

This process of splitting up is called 'polarisation'. It matters because poor people are living on housing estates that are so decrepit, vandalised and unsafe as to be below acceptable standards. It matters, too, because people living there feel helpless, looked down on by others as inferior. But polarisation is a symptom of a wider malaise afflicting British housing as a whole. Everybody's choices, not just those of low-income council tenants, are restricted at present because of fundamental flaws in the way housing is organised and financed.

In this report we examine what has been happening to council housing in Britain since 1945, and over recent decades in particular. We try to show what has gone wrong, and we discuss how to put things right.

Our report is not only about council housing but about the broader subject of social rented housing. In this context 'social' is used to mean non-profit. We say 'rented' because subsidised or other non-profit housing can be built for sale, but here we mainly use the shorter term social housing to refer to such housing for rent.

The experience of French social housing, which is organised very differently but faces many of the same problems, is drawn upon to provide a cross-national perspective. Why France? For a cross-national comparison to be of value, it needs to be of societies at a roughly similar stage of economic development and culturally similar in certain broad respects. A number of countries would obviously qualify on these grounds for comparison with Britain, France among them. It is one of Britain's nearest neighbours, a European Community partner with a similar-sized population and, at the same time, is culturally different from Britain and has experienced a more recent change from a peasant society to an advanced industrial economy.

There are also three particular reasons why we chose France. The first is that social polarisation has been recognised there, more fully than in Britain, as a major problem with social housing. The second is that the French social housing system, operated by a large number of independent agencies, provides an appropriate contrast with the arrangements currently dominant in Britain. The third is that one of us already had some knowledge of French society and French housing as a result of earlier work.[1]

British housing sectors

In Britain at present the overwhelming bulk of social housing is of course council or public housing, and in this report we often use these terms, particularly when talking about the past or about trends. But an important development in the last decade or so has been the encouragement by both Conservative and Labour governments of other forms of social housing, in particular through housing associations and, more recently, housing cooperatives. Despite their rapid growth in the last few years, housing associations do not as yet have much bearing on, for example, the comparisons over time that we draw in discussing the issue of polarisation (although their population structure is much the same as that of council housing). By 1984 housing associations still housed only 2 per cent of all households in Britain and only 7 per cent of those in social housing. In discussing the future, however, we do talk about social housing in the broader sense: a key question is how far the sector should continue, as in the past, to be mainly built, owned and managed by local authorities and how far some other forms of non-profit agency - and which forms - might take over.

Social housing obviously needs to be looked at in the wider housing context. Since the end of the Second World War the total number of dwellings in all tenures has almost doubled, while the population has increased by less than one in seven. Over the same period there has been a dramatic shift in the balance between owner-occupation, council housing and private renting. The exact figures on tenure vary according to whether one is describing the distribution of households or of dwellings - there sometimes being more than one household in a dwelling - and whether one is talking about England and Wales or Great Britain - there being proportionately more public housing in Scotland than in England and Wales. The comparisons we make are where possible between France and Great Britain, or 'Britain' as we call it throughout for simplicity; Northern Ireland is again different, with social rented housing being administered by the Northern Ireland Housing Executive instead of by local authorities.

Of all households in Britain, the proportion in owner-occupied homes has increased since 1945 from under one third to nearly two-thirds. The proportion in privately rented dwellings has fallen from half to less than one in 10. Public housing's share went up steadily in the first three decades after the war and has recently gone down because new council building has virtually ceased and because of sales to sitting tenants: the proportion of households who were its tenants, which had been about 10 per cent just before the war, rose to a peak of a third by the end of the 1970s.

Whatever efforts governments may make to revive private renting, potential landlords are likely to be sceptical about their long-term prospects compared with other ways of investing their money, and in our view unless the government engineers a major transfer of council housing to the private rented sector it is unlikely to re-establish itself as a substantial form of tenure.

The growth in owner-occupation might be restrained or increased by the actions of a future government, but the general upward trend seems set to continue at least for a while. The experience of advanced countries with high levels of home ownership - such as the United States, Australia and New Zealand - suggests, however, that it is unlikely to go higher than about 70 per cent .[2]

If these assumptions are correct, two central linked issues are raised about the future of British social housing. The first is about its share of the housing stock compared with that of owner-occupation and perhaps private renting. The second issue, already touched on, is about the form the social sector should take - what should the arrangements be for the construction, ownership and management of non-profit housing to meet the needs of those who cannot or do not wish to own their home? The second question has a bearing on the first, because the kinds of renting and the kinds of housing available in the social sector will have an impact on its scale. What happens is, however, dependent on the resources available, and these turn on the context of housing finance set by the government.

As already indicated, a distinctive characteristic of this review is that it glances at social housing on the other side of the English Channel as well as in Britain. Our aim is to gain an extra perspective by drawing on French experience.

The two systems

The French social housing system differs in important respects from the British one. Social housing in Britain is dominated by the local authorities, the other main providers being new towns and housing associations, including cooperatives. Almost all social housing in France, by contrast, is built and managed by HLM bodies (*Habitations Loyer à Modéré* or housing at moderate rents). The HLMs are more like housing associations than local authorities. Before describing in more detail the differences between the British and French systems, we need to say more about how the structure of local and regional government differs from that in Britain, because these levels of government do play a part in French housing.

The main local government bodies in France, moving upwards from the most local scale, are communes, *départements* and regions.

There are nearly 40,000 communes, alternatively described as *municipalités*, with responsibility for governing towns and rural areas; they correspond roughly to districts or boroughs in Britain. *Départements*, of which there are 94 in mainland France, roughly correspond to counties in Britain, except that their chief executive is the Prefect (*le Préfet* or, following decentralisation, *le Commissaire de la République*), who is a nominee and representative of the central government. The 21 regions, each covering up to six or seven *départements*, have clearly defined powers, for example to plan for major housing developments and to help run special schemes for priority estates.

The HLM stock is half the size of the council stock in Britain - three million dwellings compared with six million - for a similar-sized population. At the same time there are nearly 50 per cent more HLM bodies (678) than British local housing authorities (458). It follows that the average number of dwellings managed by an HLM is smaller than by a council in Britain - about 4,500 as against about 13,000.

The legal status of an HLM is different from that of a British local housing authority. Each HLM is a separate organisation, with housing powers and responsibilities only, and legally independent of both central and local government, although some HLMs are subject to local political influence. To the French this arms-length form of institution is familiar; other examples are the insurance-backed health schemes and the bodies set up to administer family allowances (the *Caisses d'Allocations Familiales*).

There are four main types of HLM. Two produce dwellings only for sale: HLM *sociétés immobiliéres*, special building societies which both finance and build homes and, much less important in scale, HLM cooperatives (for co-owners). The two main kinds of HLM whose dwellings are for rent are the *offices publics* which, as their title suggests, are public bodies, and *sociétés anonymes*, which are non-profit companies; there is also a third category - the *offices publics d'amenagement et de construction* - which are more flexible in operation than standard *offices publics* and are at present rare (only 3 per cent of all HLM renting organisations) but which, for reasons explained later, are likely to become more numerous.

5

There are more *sociétés anonymes* (56 per cent) than *offices publics* (41 per cent), but the latter have more estates and more dwellings. In the Rhone department (the one surrounding Lyons), for example, the average number of dwellings in the 18 *sociétés anonymes* is 2,600 compared with 9,900 in the six *offices publics*.[3] In France as a whole the *offices publics* own 60 per cent of the HLM stock, and they own and run the great majority of large social housing estates (the *grands ensembles*).

The HLM *sociétés anonymes* cover a wide range. Some were set up by nationalised industries to provide rented housing for their employees; examples are HLMs linked to Renault and to the Paris regional transport authority. Some were established by insurance companies or other employers, some by local chambers of commerce. Some were the creation of religious or voluntary organisations, and others provide housing for particular categories of tenants, such as ex-servicemen, large families or civil servants.

The *offices publics* are obviously the HLMs most like British local housing authorities. Such an HLM is usually chaired by the mayor (who in France is the leader and chief executive of the local council rather than the figurehead-for-a-year he or she is in Britain) or the deputy mayor, and their political influence, sometimes even their personal influence, in for example allocating dwellings can be considerable. Furthermore, in some towns - Tours is an example - the local council plays a central role in determining HLM policy. But because of the diversity, the relationships of *offices publics* with local authorities are more complex than a British model would suggest.

For one thing, most towns and rural areas do not have an *office public* at all. Take the example of the department which surrounds Lille in the industrial north of France. It has six public HLMs; one operates at departmental level, three cover the Lille conurbation itself, and two operate in other towns. Most of the industrial towns in the department have no public HLM. The Gironde, containing Bordeaux, has two - one for the whole department and one for the city. As these examples show, such public HLMs as there are do not all operate at the same geographical scale. Some are departmental, some municipal; others cover a group of municipalities or operate at a more local level - that of a district. To complicate matters still further, single estates of several thousand dwellings will often be run by a number of HLMs; in the notorious Les Minguettes in the Lyons suburbs (where riots occurred in the summer of 1981) 11 HLMs are responsible for management.[4]

Since the HLMs are independent, the local authorities are not responsible for what is done even by *office public* HLMs in their area. Until the decentralisation measures of 1982-83, HLMs could be built in a local authority area without the consent of the council; if the mayor refused to sign the authorisation the prefect, acting under the orders of the central government, would do so. That this happened quite often is shown by a statement in an English-language briefing paper, prepared by the French government in 1982 on *Implementation of Habitat Policy in France,* that HLMs 'were often forced on the local authority'.[5]

The relationship between the HLM movement and central government seems paradoxical to British eyes. In France, the *offices publics* are created by government decree. They and the *sociétés* receive the bulk of their funds for new building by means of loans through a special financial market which is subsidised by central government, with smaller amounts coming from a special pay-roll tax (the 1 per cent *patronal*) levied on firms with more than 10 employees and from the local authorities themselves. The HLMs with older property can also receive government subsidies to help pay for rehabilitation.

Apart from their financial dependence, the *offices publics* in particular are also subject to some forms of control by central government. Government representatives have to be appointed to their boards, and the *offices publics,* although they set and collect rents, do not have direct control over their own budgets; their income and expenditure are handled by the local *tresors publics,* state bodies. All HLMs are subject to inspection. And all are subject to much more control over the rents they can charge than are British councils. The rents for HLM dwellings are set between permitted minimum and maximum levels according to a regulated national scheme, and the percentage rent increases allowed each year are fixed by the government, after discussion with the HLM movement.

But if the HLMs are in some important respects more subordinate to central government than are British local authorities, they are largely independent of national party politics. Although there was a broad postwar consensus up to the 1960s in Britain about the need for a large council house building programme, and although some Conservative-controlled local authorities have recently argued for a larger council programme than the present government envisages,[6] council housing in general has been - and is - supported more strongly by Labour governments than Conservative, and Labour local authorities are, by and large, more enthusiastic about it than Conservative.

This does not apply in France. Some Right or Centre local authorities have been as keen as Left ones to support HLMs; Tours, already cited, is a case in point. At national level there was, for reasons explained in the next chapter, an across-the-board political agreement about the postwar HLM programme even more marked than the consensus in Britain. Social housing was never - and is not now - a source of party disagreement. The HLM national movement has always been able to count on a wide range of support, and it wields some influence as an independent political force.

Table 1   Housing tenure of the housing stock in Great Britain and France

column percentages

	Great Britain (Census, 1981)	France (Census, 1982)
Owner-occupied	56	51
Social housing	33	14
Privately rented	9	26
Tied to employment	2	9

Note: Social housing in Britain comprises local authority, new town and housing association; in France, HLM.

A final point is about the share of the housing stock which is rented social housing in France compared with Britain. This is shown in Table 1, which gives the patterns of tenure in the two countries at the time of the last censuses. The proportions have changed since the early 1980s; in Britain the share of owner-occupation has increased and that of social housing decreased, while in France both owner-occupation and to a lesser extent social housing have expanded. But the broad comparison holds, with the scale of social housing much smaller than in Britain, and with private landlords, though in decline in France as elsewhere, having a larger share there than in Britain.

These differences need to be borne in mind in the rest of the report, which seeks to use the comparison between the two systems as one element in the analysis of social housing's present malaise and of its possible future.

References

(1) C. Madge and P. Willmott, *Inner City Poverty in Paris and London*, London, Routledge and Kegan Paul, 1981; R. Mitton, P. Willmott and Phyllis Willmott, *Unemployment, Poverty and Social Policy: a comparative study in Britain, France and Germany*, Occasional Papers in Social Administration, London, Bedford Square Press, 1983.

(2) P. Somerville, 'Housing tenure polarisation', *Housing Review*, 35(6).

(3) *Annuaire HLM, 1987*, Paris, Union Nationale des Fédérations d'Organismes d'HLM, 1987.

(4) Ibid.

(5) Ministère de l'Urbanisme et du Logement, *Implementation of Habitat Policy in France*, Paris, Ministère de l'Urbanisme et du Logement, October 1982.

(6) Association of District Councils, *Foundations for Future Housing*, London, Association of District Councils, 1987.

2   Policies Since 1945

The role of social housing in Britain in 1939 was substantially different from what it had been at the end of the First World War. A quarter of a million slums had been demolished in the interwar years and nearly a third of a million council homes built, so that public housing's share of the total stock had risen from almost nothing to 10 per cent. But of course housing problems remained. Only half the officially-designated slums had been cleared, nearly half the dwellings in Britain lacked a fixed bath and a similar proportion were without a hot water supply.

The needs were even greater after 1945. Repairs and new house-building had been neglected in war-time, half a million homes had been destroyed or made uninhabitable by Hitler's bombs, and the population had grown by a million. Public expectations were high. In the wartime enthusiasm for postwar reconstruction, there was agreement across the political spectrum that a much larger housing programme was needed than before the war, and that the local authorities would play a key part, at least initially.

The Labour government elected in 1945 gave council housing an even more dominant role than had been envisaged in the postwar plans. The main elements of its policy were a strong emphasis on the planning of both land-use and building manpower, a large local authority-led housing programme and control, through licensing, of private (the Labour government's term was 'speculative') building. Local authority housing benefited from low-interest loans from the Public Works Loans Board and enjoyed relatively generous rates of subsidy, and the space and amenity standards were high.

In the immediate postwar years the main political debate was about the total number of new homes being built. In the 1951 General Election campaign the Conservatives promised to build 300,000 houses a year, and in the event during the early 1950s Conservative governments achieved the highest ever levels of council house building. This was done by putting pressure on local authorities to build more homes - setting them higher targets - and by reducing space and amenity standards. The dwellings built by local authorities in the 1950s were in consequence smaller and less well equipped than those built in the 1940s - a change which did not begin to be reversed until after the Parker Morris Report in 1961, and then only slowly. It was not until 1967 that the subsidy system was based on the higher space and amenity standards recommended by Parker Morris.

From 1954 to 1964 the main impact of Conservative governments on public housing was to reduce its role. They encouraged private building for sale and tried to revive the private rented sector, in particular by encouraging 'more realistic' rents. More important, once the 300,000 target was reached - in 1953 - the government argued that local authorities should now confine themselves to slum clearance. As Harold Macmillan put it in 1954: 'Local authorities and local authorities alone can clear and rehouse the slums, while the general housing need can be met, as it was to a great extent before the war, by private enterprise'.[1] The general needs housing subsidy was abolished and central government subsidies were provided only for slum clearance and housing for elderly people. (Though a general subsidy was reintroduced in 1961, it was then only for local authorities charging high rents, and mainly benefited rural councils rather than the urban ones with the biggest housing problems.) In 1955 local authorities were denied access to low-interest capital; the government directed them to use the money market rather than the Public Works Loans Board.

Thus the first two decades after 1945 - up to the election of the first Wilson government in 1964 - can be seen as influenced by party political philosophies: five years in which public housing was favoured, followed by 13 years in which it was gradually relegated to second place.

The rise and fall of high rise

The term 'mass housing' has been coined for 'large flatted estates of uniform housing',[2] the most characteristic form being high rise, defined as five storeys or over but often much higher. Even at their peak high flats and other mass housing accounted for a minority of the council homes being built. Currently, flats of all types account for only one third of all the council stock, and those in blocks of five storeys or more for only about a twelfth. But the absolute number of such homes is still substantial; getting on for half a million British households live in high rise blocks.

The high rise boom deserves special attention as an influential episode in the postwar history of public housing in Britain. There were several unusual features. For one thing the policy as a whole was never really made explicit, nor debated until after it had run its course. Secondly, it was in effect bipartisan - backed for most of the period by an alliance between a Conservative central government and the predominantly Labour-controlled cities, with the Labour Opposition at Westminster passive in its acceptance - but again this was not explicitly acknowledged.

Apart from small schemes on bombed sites, most council housing in the immediate postwar period had been low rise (including some non-traditional types of construction) on estates outside the towns and cities. This was, rightly, seen as the best way to provide new homes quickly, and the policy was continued later through the new towns and later still the 'expanded towns'. The switch of emphasis to local authority slum clearance in the late 1950s turned attention to the inner areas where most of the slums were.

Most of the new council housing in such areas during this period was in the form of flats, and much of it was high rise. Table 2, which is reproduced from Cooney's analysis of the 'rise and decline' of high flats[3] shows that flats of five storeys and over accounted for only 7 per cent of public housing approvals in England and Wales in the period from 1953 to 1959. By 1966 their share had risen to a peak of 26 per cent. The tallest blocks, 15 storeys and over, amounted to about 10 per cent of all public housing tenders approved in the three years 1965, 1966 and 1967.

Table 2   **The rise and decline of the high flat: tenders approved for local authorities and new towns in England and Wales by storey heights as percentage of all dwellings approved**

	5-14 (A)	15 & over (B)	A+B	Number of dwellings
1953 to 1959	6.4	0.5	6.9	971,678
1960 to 1964	12.3	7.0	19.3	595,403
1965	10.9	10.6	21.5	162,540
1966	15.3	10.4	25.7	172,557
1967	13.3	9.7	23.0	170,545
1968	14.0	5.9	19.9	154,308
1969	9.7	3.8	13.5	112,201
1970	8.0	1.8	9.8	98,080

The period was relatively short, the reaction setting in well before the Ronan Point disaster in 1968. Two key questions are raised: first, why did the high rise boom occur, despite the consistent evidence from opinion polls that most people disliked flats and high flats above all; secondly, why did the decline set in?

It seems that a number of contributory elements came together at the same time. One was the shared progressive vision that had taken shape during the war. The first aim of environmental planning was to put right what were seen as the mistakes of the interwar period, with deepening slums inside the cities and mushrooming suburban 'sprawl' outside them. The new policy was to contain the spread of the cities and, inside urban areas, to clear the slums and replace them with more spacious and better equipped homes in the setting of a more attractive environment.

This approach seemed at the time to lead to a clear and logically irresistible set of planning principles for dealing with the cities and older industrial towns. The first step was to promote 'comprehensive redevelopment': the temptation to piecemeal treatment had to be resisted; large areas needed to be cleared, the rows of little streets demolished, in order to make possible the clean sweep that was needed. Then, so the argument went, if densities were to be high enough to provide for all those needing to live in the towns and cities, the physical form needed to be 'mixed development', with large proportions of flats, rather than houses. As time went on, the emphasis was on more flats and on high flats in particular.

As well as the planning philosophy developed in wartime, a number of other influences were at work. Demographic trends were among them. The population projections were of 52 million in 1961, 60 million in 1981 and 70 million in 2001, and there was serious concern over a future national land shortage.

Then there was the dominance of the so-called 'modern movement' in architecture, and in particular the ideas of Le Corbusier, whose vision of 'cities in the air' inspired two generations of British architects, including the architect-planners and other officials in the key central and local government posts during the period.

The architects' desire to build high seemed to fit in with the bipartisan wartime reaction against the urban sprawl of the 1930s and anxieties about the consequences of a population explosion. As inner area redevelopment got under way, government subsidy policy supported the new thinking. Building high was more expensive and the government assumption was that local authorities needed financial incentives to do it. As well as receiving subsidies to buy expensive urban building land, councils were first given a larger subsidy if they built flats rather than houses and, from 1956 on, a subsidy that went up with the height of the block.

Another important influence was the development of industrialised building, using methods imported from France and other continental countries such as Sweden and Holland. These were said to be cheaper and faster than traditional methods. Industrialised building techniques would help to overcome the problems created by a shortage of building industry craftsmen, which was assumed to be a crucial bottleneck in the 1950s and 1960s. Although the new 'systems' were used for low rise as well, their discovery coincided with the enthusiasm in Britain for high rise, and the new methods were increasingly promoted by the large contracting firms as the solution for inner city and, as time went on, even suburban housing.

Most politicians of both Left and Right welcomed the new housing forms. This was, as already suggested, partly because of the general desire - in response to public pressure - to build substantial numbers of homes, and build them quickly. Looking back in 1973 to the period when he had been Minister of Housing (1962-64), Sir Keith Joseph agonised, 'I suppose that I was genuinely convinced that I had a new answer. It was prefabrication and, Heaven help me, high blocks'.[4] At the local level the policy was encouraged by the persuasiveness of the council planners, who were predominantly architect-planners, but also by the PR methods used by the big contracting firms. Councillors were feted and entertained on high-powered visits to model schemes, including some in Denmark, Holland and France. Dunleavy quotes a councillor who was one of a party taken by a contractor in a bus to see some of his new flats in a nearby town; there were drinks in a marquee at the beginning and end of the visit, after which the council ordered five blocks, 'as if we were buying bags of sweets'.[5]

Despite the arguments in favour of high rise, in practice it had little in its favour. Though there were honourable exceptions, most of the postwar blocks of flats, high and low alike, were so barrack-like - so much the image of mass housing - that they made the councils' prewar neo-georgian blocks and cottage estates seem handsome by comparison. Because of the space needed around the buildings to reduce overshadowing, little land was actually saved. In any case the fears of land shortage inside the cities were unfounded. People were already migrating from the cities, not only to new towns but also - and to a much greater extent - to private suburban housing, and the pressures in the cities were therefore less than was supposed.

The new industrialised methods were largely untried, at least in a British context. While not all blocks were badly designed or built, many were. There were countless design flaws, large and small; site supervision was frequently inadequate; and the work was often incompetently carried out. Together these failings account for the disproportionate numbers of faults needing attention and the high outstanding lists of repairs and maintenance needed in the blocks of that period.

Furthermore, the new forms of housing turned out to be more expensive, not less; flats cost about half as much again as two-storey houses. They did not even prove quicker to build, consistently taking longer to complete for occupation, partly because the first family could not move in until the whole block was ready. Because of problems of design and insulation they also often proved expensive to heat. Inadequate and unreliable lifts were another problem.

The drawbacks of the flatted blocks were compounded by poor housing management. Tenants in such accommodation were more dependent than others on effective management, and often found it difficult to get prompt action when their flat was infested with cockroaches, when the windows jammed or the walls ran with water, or when the too-narrow rubbish chutes overflowed. Local housing management, and the response to minor crises in particular, could no doubt have been improved on 'cottage estates' and on estates of conventional low rise flats, but the problems were now multiplied, partly by the greater incidence of things going wrong, partly by the scale of the estates, and partly by a growing tendency, from the early 1960s on, to abolish resident caretakers on grounds of cost and efficiency. The combination of design requiring a high level of management with a local authority management system which was often ineffective even in delivering basic repairs posed more problems than had ever emerged with traditional building.

High rise had always had its critics, but from the mid-1960s the complaints mounted. Some local authorities, including Birmingham for example, reported that they were beginning to find it difficult to let their high flats. At about the same time, MPs (who until then had shown little interest) and Ministers became concerned. Tenants were increasingly expressing their unhappiness, particularly those with children, and it began to be realised that, although high flats were unsuitable for such families, many were living in them.

Neither then nor since has tenant discontent with high rise been uniform. High blocks with family-sized flats and slab or deck access blocks have generally proved the most unpopular and most difficult to let. It has always been easier to find tenants for blocks with smaller flats and 'point' blocks which are easier to make secure and to manage effectively; such flats are also easier to refurbish and convert, for example into semi-sheltered housing for elderly people.

As well as the reaction to high rise on social grounds - reflecting the general unpopularity of flats - other objections began to be raised. The saving of land that could be achieved by building at high density was questioned by economists and geographers. Architectural opinion too began to turn; in 1968 the then President of the Royal Institute of British Architects wrote about 'a sea of concrete and asphalt ... The crude visual impact of many of these developments on our city skyline is already apparent'.[6]

These anxieties were matched by growing government concern about costs. A partial switch of government subsidy away from high rise envisaged by the Labour Government before the 1966 General Election and introduced in April 1967 was followed by the imposition of cost yardsticks which worked against high building. The reduction of the public spending programme after devaluation in 1967 - leading to a reduction in public authority housing for several years - made expensive high rise building even less attractive.

Thus, just as a combination of influences had worked to encourage high flats, so a decade later a different combination began to move against them. The revolt by tenants, a growing awareness of the social and aesthetic disadvantages, scepticism about savings in land, faults of design and construction, problems of maintenance and management, and concern about costs - all these worked in the same direction.

There is now general recognition that the high rise phase was a collective aberration. As many as 10,000 of the homes built in the 1950s and 1960s have now been demolished. Among those that remain, many could be made attractive and acceptable. It is of course true that in some of the council stock built in other periods as well there are blocks nobody wants to live in and backlogs of repairs. But the mass housing boom has left a disproportionate legacy of problems. The Audit Commission, analysing 'the crisis in council housing', argued that the period had produced much of 'the wrong type of housing', mentioned 'design faults (e.g. flat roofs, problems with deck access), and problems with new materials and non-traditional methods', and added that 'many local authorities' estates, accounting for as much as 30 per cent of their stock in some cases, are now classified as "difficult to let"...'[7]

The dominance of mass housing over less than two decades was more influential than might be suggested by the scale. Despite the abandonment of the policy 20 years ago, and despite the demolitions, the physical presence of the blocks still dominates the landscape of most British towns and cities. The episode continues to be invoked as an example of the arrogance of architects and town planners, and at least partly explains the low reputation of those professions. Furthermore, Dunleavy was surely right in his suggestion that 'the high-rise housing boom cast a sizeable blight on the public image of post-war council housing', illustrating as it did in the public eye 'the inherent inefficiency, bureaucratic indifference, and unresponsiveness of state intervention compared with market provision'.[8]

It would, of course, be misleading to see council housing as split between a uniform traditional sector of houses with gardens on the one hand and systems-built mass housing on the other. There are low rise non-traditional forms, including some which also suffer from severe repair and maintenance problems, and there are other differences of design, location and management. The difficult to let and difficult to manage estates are not all high rise. There are a range of differences in standards and reputation between estates, reflecting when they were built, who has lived in them and how they have been used and managed. The differences also reflect local social and economic circumstances, past decisions to accept or refuse offers of tenancies and decisions to move away.

But it remains true that much of the mass housing provides poor homes by virtually all standards other than the level of internal amenities. The public sector stock as a whole can be seen as a series of strata, each reflecting the legislation and policies of their period. In these terms, the homes of the mass housing era represent one of the low points - perhaps the lowest point - in nearly a century of public housing.

Financial pressures and owner-occupation
Concern with the finances of social housing has preoccupied goverments of both Left and Right since the late 1960s. Though there have been some differences according to the political complexion of the central government over this period, the common themes are more striking.

The devaluation of 1967 has already been mentioned as leading to changes in the subsidy arrangements for public sector housing. Over much of the period since then, worries about the state of the economy and about the growing burdens imposed by the changing age structure of the population have led to successive attempts to contain public spending in general and that on public housing in particular. Finance has come more and more to dominate housing policy. Deficit subsidies linked to cost controls and cash limits have replaced the flat rate dwelling subsidies which had been the norm in council housing's earlier years.

A second bipartisan approach has been an emphasis on rehabilitation rather than redevelopment and new building, though here Labour governments have put more emphasis on municipalisation (for example in Housing Action Areas in the cities) and Conservative governments on rehabilitating privately-owned property. Rehabilitation was embraced partly in reaction against the experience of slum clearance and mass housing. It was increasingly recognised that wholesale redevelopment had broken up established communities and imposed heavy social costs, and also that the time was now ripe to improve and modernise old property rather than go on building new.

In addition the House Condition Survey of 1967 had shown that large numbers of dwellings needing attention were outside clearance and potential clearance areas, and included an increasing proportion of owner-occupied dwellings. 'As the very very worst houses were cleared the remaining poor-quality houses were more widely dispersed around the inner city and not so amenable to the concentrated area approach of redevelopment'.[9] The new policy also reflected the growing concern with costs. Rehabilitation was seen as an alternative to clearance and redevelopment, and one which was less expensive financially as well as socially.

A third and increasingly important theme since the 1960s has been government support for owner-occupation at the expense of council housing. A series of government measures have made owner-occupation more attractive. The encouragements to home ownership included the abolition in 1962 of Schedule A tax (on the notional rent of owner-occupied homes) and the development in 1967 of the Option Mortgage Scheme, giving the equivalent of income tax relief to people who did not earn enough to pay tax. All this has led to a growing bill for mortgage tax relief, which has risen with increasing incomes, house prices and interest rates.

The largely bipartisan character of support for owner-occupation was shown in the way the 1977 Labour Green Paper on *Housing Policy* so closely echoed the Conservative White Paper of a few years earlier. The Conservative Conservative Government had said 'Home ownership... satisfies a deep and natural desire...', the Labour Government that 'owning one's home is a basic and natural desire'.[10] The promise by Anthony Crosland (Secretary of State for the Environment in the mid 1970s) of a fundamental restructuring of housing finance was abandoned for a set of proposals which would continue to support owner-occupation through tax relief but would restrain the otherwise-inevitable growth in public housing. The proposed new system for financing council housing 'gave local authorities some flexibility but introduced a strong element of central government control'.[11] This operated through project and cash controls rather than specific limits on the number of dwellings built.

The three Conservative governments since 1979 have in one sense continued the policies proposed by their Labour predecessor, but have intensified the pressures against council housing. In the 1980 Housing Act, the government introduced the new subsidy arrangements proposed in the 1977 Green Paper, but in a form which shifted more control than Labour had envisaged from the the local authorities to central government.

The impact on public housing of the various cutbacks can readily be shown by a few figures, all as it happens for England. Local authority new housing completions fell from 105,000 in 1976 to 67,000 in 1979 and 22,000 in 1985. With the growth in council house sales the local authority sector began to decline in size from 1980. Following the 1980 Housing Act council rents in general increased sharply until 1983. Because of these various changes the Exchequer subsidy for council housing was reduced from £1,393 million in 1980-81 to £379 million in 1984-85.

The cuts in subsidy and investment in council housing have been much larger than in any other public service. In terms of expenditure on housing as a whole, there has been a switch in expenditure away from council housing and towards housing benefit, housing associations and owner-occupation; the last of these has increased because of the growing government bill for tax reliefs of various kinds enjoyed by home owners and because of higher discounts to encourage council tenants to buy.

The French postwar experience

The postwar history of housing in France can be seen as falling into three phases. In the period from 1945 to 1953, the priority in official policy was to transform the economy, so the main emphasis was on investment in industry. Housing in general and social housing in particular received little government attention. Only 500,000 homes were built - a third of the number in Britain during the same period for a similar sized population.

The second phase was dominated by the large-scale expansion of HLM housing. In the early 1950s the government began to recognise that, as part of its postwar economic development - in which France was belatedly emulating its already industrialised neighbours in northern Europe - it needed to change from an agricultural to an industrial economy, from a rural to an urban society. What was required therefore was a rapid and substantial programme of urban housing in the areas where the new industries were developing. Homes were needed for a rapidly growing economy and for its new labour force, as well as for a rapidly growing total population.[12]

Hence the government's HLM programme. Social housing had existed before the war but had been of only minor importance - in 1950 the total number of HLM dwellings was less than 200,000. The HLM programme was widely seen as a necessary response to the needs of the times, and this helps to explain the bipartisan support referred to in the previous chapter.

The HLMs were created and financed by the government, to implement the national house-building programme. The housing could be built where the government decided it was needed and, thanks to the injection of public money, the choice of green-field sites and the use of new industrialised methods, it could be built quickly. But neither central government itself nor the local authorities would build or manage the new housing.

In terms of numbers the programme was a great success. France's total housing output rose from 120,000 dwellings in 1953 to 300,000 a year by the late 1950s and 500,000 a year by the end of the 1960s. About a third of these were HLM, the great majority of them for rent rather than sale.

New administrative arrangements were introduced at various stages to promote faster building and, in the larger schemes, to try to create planned communities with adequate services rather than gigantic dormitories lacking facilities, as some of the earlier estates were. The two main instruments, employed in the context of regional plans for housing development, were the ZUPs (*Zones d'Urbanisation Prioritaire*) from 1958 and the ZACs (*Zones d'Aménagement Concerté*) from 1967. By 1985 the Zones accounted for a quarter of all HLM dwellings.[13]

The Zones, developed by local authorities or mixed bodies on which public interests predominated, also contain the great majority of the *grands ensembles,* the large estates, those with about 1,000 or more dwellings, which were mainly built in the HLM boom of the 1950s and 1960s. No firm figures are available, but it is estimated that about a third of all HLM dwellings - a total of one million - are in *grands ensembles.*[14]

The *grands ensembles* were, and are, mass housing (*urbanisme de masse*), and in general a much larger proportion of French postwar social housing than British was built in flatted form. As in Britain, however, flats and particularly those in *tours* (towers) and *barres* (slabs) have, because of their unpopularity and their other problems, been discouraged since the late 1960s. Of HLM dwellings built before 1967, 95 per cent are flats, compared with 80 per cent built since then. But 90 per cent of existing HLM dwellings are still flats,[15] compared with the third or so of social housing in Britain which is flats or maisonettes, and of course the *grands ensembles* survive.

The third phase of French postwar housing policy, which began in the 1970s, was one in which the HLMs began to face growing financial problems and, at the same time, the government gave more and more support to private construction and to home ownership. The financial crisis of the HLMs resulted from the familiar problem of their trying to keep rents at an affordable level while ensuring adequate funds for the maintenance and modernisation that were becoming increasingly necessary. By 1975 it was evident that urgent action was needed, and in that year two official reports - one on the HLMs in particular and the other on the reform of housing subsidies - proposed that HLM rents should be increased and at the same time public financial support given to households to enable them to pay the increased rents.[16] These proposals were implemented in the French Housing Act of 1977. From then on, as in Britain from a rather earlier date, the emphasis was on subsidising people rather than buildings.

Under the 1977 Act households v 'th inc.. es below a specified level could receive a new benefit - *Aide Personnalisée au Logement* (APL). For HLM tenants this arrangement was dependent on the HLM entering into an agreement (a *convention*) with the government to receive a new subsidy towards the cost of rehabilitation and at the same time agreeing to raise rents, a substantial proportion of the higher rent for poorer tenants being met by the APL. This form of personal support was available for people buying their home as well as for HLM tenants, and the cost of subsidising house purchasers through the APL is more than double that for tenants.

The 1977 legislation made it possible for the HLM organisations to increase their income and carry out essential rehabilitation, and it encouraged the growth of owner-occupation. But it created an anomaly within HLM housing. A two-tier system of housing benefit developed, with one type - the APL - available to all HLM tenants in rehabilitated properties who had low incomes, and the other - the AL (*Allocations de Logement*) - at lower rates and available only to tenants receiving family allowances or in other special categories, for example elderly people and the long-term unemployed.

From January 1988, however, HLMs have been able to enter into *conventions* without carrying out rehabilitation. They agree to raise their rents, and at the same time their tenants become eligible for APL 2 (at the AL rates) on the basis of their household income alone. This new system is expected to be implemented over three or four years. The reform has if anything added to the government's continuing worry over the rising cost of housing benefit for HLM tenants.

As for the growth of home ownership, this began in the mid-1960s, but official recognition of a policy to give it substantial support was not made explicit until the same Housing Act of 1977. Since then, in France as in Britain, owner-occupation has continued to grow rapidly.

Conclusion

In comparing the postwar experience of Britain and France, the main interest is in, first, the period of mass housing in both countries - from the mid-1950s to the mid-1960s - and, second, the problems with which the sector in each country now has to deal. The second set of issues are taken up later; the first deserve some attention as part of this brief historical review.

There were some differences. One is that, despite the large French programme after 1953, social housing accounts for a smaller proportion of the total stock in France than in Britain. Another difference is that flats, mass housing and in particular the *grands ensembles* constitute a larger proportion of the total stock of social housing in France than in the British social housing stock. Yet another is that a much larger proportion of HLM housing than of British social housing is on the outskirts of towns and cities, though the emphasis has been recently changing somewhat in France (much later than in Britain) towards the redevelopment and rehabilitation of housing, mainly privately-owned, in inner areas.

Despite these contrasts, mass housing is in both countries the dominant symbol of postwar social housing - and of what went wrong with it. The same questions can therefore be asked about why things happened as they did.

The starting point was certainly different in the two countries. For one thing, flats were much more in tune with the French urban tradition than the English (the Scots being in this more like the French than the English). The contrast with the continent was pointed out by Rasmussen in 1934:

> Two chief types are distinguished among large cities: the concentrated and the scattered. The former is the more common on the Continent and is clearly represented in the big government seats of Paris and Vienna ... The second type is represented by the English town ... the English example is amazing, for their great industrial cities, in which each family has its own house, have been created without any difficulty - and London, the largest city in the world, is the very type of the scattered city.[17]

The French housing system has not readily lent itself to construction in any form other than flats on the one hand and *maisons individuelles* (single-family houses) on the other; there are few of the semis and terraces so common in Britain. High flats in particular were encouraged after 1953 in France, as in Britain from about the same date, partly because of the influence of the architectural 'modern movement', and partly because of the desire for high density (though the French, building on green field sites, had less need of it). Industrialised building systems were adopted in France because of the emphasis on speed and because the methods were in any event more advanced there; indeed, British councillors were often persuaded to embrace the new systems after their visits to model French HLM schemes.

The reason for the very different location - on the edges of cities rather than inside them - was again speed. Once the government-promoted HLM programme was launched, it was important to acquire sites quickly and start building without delay. The aim at that stage was not the redevelopment of inner areas but the rapid creation of a large additional stock of new homes to meet the needs of the economy and the growing population. The large and accessible sites that were required, particularly for the ZUPs and ZACs, were unlikely to be found inside the towns or cities.

These differences notwithstanding, both countries were alike in the enthusiasm with which systems methods were used to build high rise blocks for urban social housing in the 1950s and 1960s. It seems that, in France as in Britain, there was during the same two decades a similar convergence of architectural fashion, technical development, pressure from the construction industry and political conviction leading to large scale mass housing estates.

If there are similarities in that period, there are also similarities in what has happened since. Two trends are particularly important. First, in France as in Britain, economic and financial worries have put increasing pressure on the social housing sector, have constrained its development and generated governmental concern about the costs of subsidising low-income tenants. Second, in France and Britain alike, owner-occupation is the expanding form of tenure. For the two countries these trends are partly reflections, partly causes, of the problems which are the subject of the rest of this report.

References

(1) Harold Macmillan in 1954, quoted R. Samuel, J. Kincaid and E. Slater, 'But nothing happens', in 'The long pursuit: studies in the government's slum clearance programme', *New Left Review*, 1962, 13-14, p. 55.

(2) P. Dunleavy, *The Politics of Mass Housing in Britain, 1945-1975,* Oxford, Clarendon Press, 1981, p.1.

(3) E.W. Cooney, 'High flats in local authority housing in England and Wales', in A. Sutcliffe (ed), *Multi-Storey Living*, London, Croom Helm, 1974, pp.151-80; table on p.152.

(4) Dunleavy, op.cit., p.170.

(5) Ibid., p.285.

(6) Sir Hugh Wilson, quoted in Cooney, op. cit., p.173.

(7) Audit Commission for Local Authorities in England and Wales, *Managing the Crisis in Council Housing*, London, HMSO, 1986, p.5.

(8) P. Dunleavy, op.cit., p.355.

(9) J.R. Short, *Housing in Britain,* London, Methuen, 1982, p.58.

(10) Both quoted in Short, ibid., p.60 and p.62.

(11) Ibid., p.63.

(12) This has been pointed out by Harloe. See, for example, M. Harloe, 'The declining fortunes of social housing in Europe', in D. Clapham and J. English (editors), *Public Housing: Current Trends and Future Developments,* London, Croom Helm, 1987, pp. 126-44.

(13) Direction de la Construction, Paris, unpublished analyses of national HLM survey carried out in 1985.

(14) Estimate by Union Nationale des Fédérations d'Organismes d'HLM, Paris, personal communication.

(15) Direction de la Construction, op.cit.

(16) The reports are the 'Livre Blanc', Tome 1 of 'Propositions Pour l'Habitat', *Revue HLM*, No. 244 Supp., 1975, Paris, Union Nationale des Fédérations d'Organismes d'HLM and the Barre Report on housing finance, *Rapport de la Commision d'Etudes d'une Réforme du Financement de Logement*, Présidée par Raymond Barre, Paris, La Documentation Francaise, 1976.

(17) S. Rasmussen, *London: the Unique City*, Cambridge Massachusetts, MIT Press, 1982, pp. 23-4.

3   Polarisation Between Tenures

In recent decades there have been important changes in the population
structure of council housing and of other tenures, summed up in the
term social polarisation. These trends are the subject of this chapter and
the next, and they are linked to the other problems discussed in the
following chapter. In Britain, though social polarisation has received
some attention from housing specialists and researchers, there is little
public debate about it, and it does not figure on the agenda of either
government or opposition parties. This relative neglect contrasts with
France, where the changes in the social mix of the population are
recognised as important causes of the crisis facing some of the larger
HLM estates built in the 1950s and 1960s.

To say that social polarisation is occurring in Britain can mean two
different propositions: that social housing increasingly contains
low-status, poor and disadvantaged people, and that such people are
increasingly concentrated in particular areas and estates. The first
dimension, polarisation between tenures, is explored in this chapter; the
second, polarisation within social housing, in the next.

Such processes of change can be measured in a variety of ways,
using a range of indices. We draw upon a number of analyses that have
been made and add some of our own. The comparisons obviously
depend on the availability of the figures, and the geographical area used
is not always the same; sometimes it is the United Kingdom, sometimes
Britain, sometimes England and Wales, often just England.

Even in comparing trends between sectors, an initial distinction
has to be made between what is happening within the council sector as

compared with other sectors - is there, for instance, an increasing proportion among council tenants of people who are in low-skill occupations? - and what is happening within a particular group - is an increasing proportion of all low-skill people, to continue the example, living in council housing? The broad conclusions are often the same, but the picture can look different, particularly if the numbers of households in the categories are small or if they have changed over time. We do not always present the data both ways round, but we have taken the problem into account as far as possible in what we report.

As we have already suggested, our analyses in these two chapters are mainly of what has been happening to the social structure of council housing, not of social housing in general. Fewer figures are available for the (much smaller) housing association sector. But such evidence as there is can be briefly summarised. Housing associations have slightly lower proportions than does council housing of people with limited job skills and of households with low incomes. They have slightly higher proportions of people who are outside the labour market and of elderly people. In general the social structures of the two sectors are broadly similar. What is more, the trends in both have been similar in recent years.[1]

Social status and income

Changes in the occupational structures of different tenures in England and Wales between the 1961, 1971 and 1981 Censuses were examined by Hamnett.[2] As he explains, the validity of the comparisons between 1971 and 1981 is weakened by changes in the classification of occupations; the main relevant change was a down-grading of some non-manual jobs and a consequential small increase in the numbers classified as in the semi-skilled groups (semi-skilled manual workers and personal service workers). These problems are however, as Hamnett put it, unlikely 'to negate either the general pattern of changes or the conclusions'.

The analysis shows that the proportion of the unskilled heads of household who were in council housing was 39 per cent in 1961, 49 per cent in 1971 and 56 per cent in 1981. Among semi-skilled and personal service workers, the proportions at the three dates were 32 per cent, 39 per cent and 42 per cent. So the proportions of both these groups who were in public housing increased over the 20-year period - and, as the figures suggest, did so rather more between 1961 and 1971 than between 1971 and 1981.

Comparisons the other way round - of the proportions of public housing tenants at different dates - are complicated by changes not just in the classification of jobs but also in the occupational structure itself. For these analyses Hamnett compared only 1961 and 1981, presumably because of the technical complexity. The first change was an increase in the number of 'economically inactive' household heads (that is, those who were neither working nor seeking work), which rose from 7 per cent of all household heads in 1961 to 19 per cent in 1981; this affected the comparisons because it drastically reduced the numbers in the other categories - those remaining in the labour force.

Secondly, among those who were economically active there were changes in the proportions in the different socio-economic categories, reflecting changes in the economy. Over the 20-year period the total number of households in England and Wales headed by skilled manual workers fell by 7 per cent, those headed by semi-skilled by 3 per cent (despite the small increase as a result of the changes in classification) and those headed by unskilled by 24 per cent. The proportions of non-manual, and particularly professional and managerial, heads of households increased correspondingly. Given these national changes, the best one can do, as Hamnett did, is to present two sets of percentages, first with the economically inactive left out of the total and then with them included alongside the low-skill people; the argument for using this particular combination, rather than putting the economically inactive with another group, is that the great majority of economically inactive people were, like low-skill people, sure to have been relatively disadvantaged - as retired people, widows or lone parents.

Among the economically active first of all, the proportion of household heads in the council sector who were semi-skilled (again including personal service workers) and unskilled rose from 37 per cent in 1961 to 39 per cent in 1981. Thus there were more such people in public housing at the later date despite the sizeable fall in the total numbers of people in such jobs. Second, with the economically inactive included, the proportion of council tenants who were semi-skilled, unskilled or outside the labour force was 40 per cent in 1961 and 56 per cent in 1981. These figures again confirm that council housing contained larger proportions of low-skill/low-status people at the later date.

Income is in some ways a more relevant measure, particularly for testing the proposition that public housing contains more of the poor than it did. Calculations by Somerville based on the Family Expenditure Survey show that the proportion of the poorest 10 per cent of households in Britain who were in council housing went up from 33 per cent in 1968 to 56 per cent in 1978 and 58 per cent in 1983.[3]

The Somerville analysis can be reworked to answer the question about how far council housing contained more poor people. Detailed examination showed that households divided fairly clearly into three groups - the poorest 30 per cent, who accounted for an increasing share of public housing; the middle 20 per cent, whose share stayed the same at the three dates; and the richest half, who figured in the sector to a decreasing extent (Table 3).

Table 3   Income of households in council housing (Great Britain)

column percentages

	1968	1978	1983
Proportion of council housing tenants who were among the:			
Poorest 30 per cent of all households	31	42	52
Middle 20 per cent of all households	23	23	23
Richest 50 per cent of all households	46	35	25

Source: Family Expenditure Surveys in Somerville, 1986.

The table shows that, whereas in 1968 the proportion of the poorest households in council housing closely reflected their proportion in the country as a whole (31 per cent of tenants from among the poorest 30 per cent of households), their share had increased by 1978 and had by 1983 gone up further to account for over half the council stock. Conversely, the share of council housing taken up by the richest half of households fell from not much short of a half to just over a third in 1978 and a quarter in 1983.

In terms of earnings, calculations from New Earnings Survey and General Household Survey data show that those of male council tenants in full-time work were in 1981 and 1984 lower than the average earnings of all men in full-time work, and that the gap widened between the two dates.[4]

Other evidence shows that over a quarter of a century there has been a decline in the numbers of households in public housing containing earners. The proportion of households in the public sector with no earners at all rose from 11 per cent in 1962 to 23 per cent in 1971, 30 per cent in 1978 and 44 per cent in 1982, as against 16 per cent, 22 per cent, 25 per cent and 30 per cent among all tenures.[5] Thus, in a period when the proportion of no-earner households in general roughly doubled, the increase within council housing was four-fold.

A related measure of income is whether a household has multiple earners, households with two or more earners generally being relatively well-off. Among all households, the proportion of them fell slightly from 42 per cent in 1962 to 37 per cent in 1982; in council housing the proportion dropped from 55 per cent to 26 per cent over the same period.[6] So, again, at the later date the sector contained a smaller share than other tenures of the better-off households.

A further index of relative prosperity or poverty is the proportion of families receiving supplementary benefit; since this is the support provided by the Department of Health and Social Security for people who are without an adequate income, an increase in the proportion of recipients who are in council housing would be another indication that the sector contained more poor people. There has been a long term trend from as long ago as 1954. Over the following three decades or so the total number of households in Great Britain receiving supplementary benefit (or its predecessor, national assistance) increased to more than double what it had been (1954, 1.4 million; 1983, 3.2 million). But the number of all receiving households who were living in public housing increased - nearly seven fold (1954, 0.3 million; 1983, 2.0 million).[7]

A related point is about housing benefits. Because of changes over time in the way households get official help with their rents, it is not easy to calculate how the different sectors have fared historically. But government figures show that, despite the reduction in the scale of council housing, the number of tenants in Britain receiving such help increased by over a third between 1980 and 1986; by mid-1987 as many as 63 per cent of council tenants were getting it.[8]

Unemployment

Among the other dimensions related to tenure, one is unemployment. Many more council tenants are unemployed than are people in other tenures. The Labour Force Survey showed that in England the proportion of household heads who were out of work in 1984 was nearly six times as high among council tenants as among owner-occupiers. What is more, the proportion increased between 1977-78 and 1984 by 88 per cent among council tenants, compared with 58 per cent among owner-occupiers.[9]

Such variations might simply have been a reflection of the greater propensity to unemployment in the low-skill jobs in which, as we have shown, council tenants are increasingly concentrated. But in the same survey there were similar differences by tenure when people's occupations were held constant.[10] As Holmans shows, drawing on other data, geographical variations in unemployment are not the explanation either: 'Unemployment rates ... differed between tenures in a way that could not be explained by regional differences in unemployment rates and in tenures'.[11] Thus, though variations in the occupational structures of tenures or areas may explain some of the difference in unemployment rates between council tenants and owner-occupiers, substantial differences remain.

Murphy and Sullivan's analysis of the 1981 Labour Force Survey focussed on unemployed males between school leaving age and 30.[12] They found that unemployment rates were two or three times higher among those in local authority accommodation than those in owner-occupation, with rates in other tenures falling between. The differences by tenure were comparable in scale to those by other characteristics which might be expected to be directly related to the employment market - occupational status and educational achievement. The analysis also showed marked differences in unemployment rates by tenure within occupational and educational categories and within broad geographical areas.

Murphy and Sullivan suggest that these patterns reflect the effect of unemployment on patterns of household formation and vice versa, and the possible movement of unemployed people into council housing. Among married male heads of household aged 16 to 49, those who had moved into council housing were about six times more likely to be unemployed than were those who had moved into owner-occupation. It also appeared that the long-term unemployed in particular moved into council housing.

Other kinds of polarisation
Successive General Household Surveys show the proportions of people in Britain of different ages according to tenure. In 1971 15 per cent of all household heads in the general population were aged 70 or over; the proportion of heads of that age in council housing was the same - 15 per cent. By 1977 their proportion in the general population was 18 per cent and in council housing 21 per cent, and in 1984 20 per cent and 27 per cent respectively. So over time the gap had widened: public housing increasingly contains more of the nation's elderly people.

This change partly reflects when estates were built, the peak period having been the 1950s and 1960s when today's 70 year olds were in their 30s and 40s; many of them have continued to live where they were. It also reflects the general process through which people with lower incomes are 'filtered' towards council housing. Since older people have lower incomes on average, more often have no earners in the household, and are more likely than members of other types of household to draw supplementary benefit, the age trend is obviously linked to others already reported.

Marital status is linked to age, and it is no surprise that council housing contains a larger proportion of widows and widowers than does owner-occupation. It also contains a larger proportion of divorced and separated people.[13] This is partly explained by the fact that people who marry young more often go into council housing and also divorce more often. But Murphy and Sullivan showed that, even taking marriage age into account, there were proportionately more divorced people among council tenants than owner-occupiers.[14]

Some of the divorced and separated people have children. The total number of single-parent households, as a proportion of all households, increased from 2 per cent in 1961 to 5 per cent in 1983. Such families are more likely than two-parent families to have low incomes and limited resources, and so more of them find their way into council housing. An important influence has been the Housing (Homeless Persons) Act of 1977, under which parents with dependent children constitute the main priority group for local authority housing. More and more of the new entrants into council housing are homeless families: in England and Wales the number went up from 43,000 in 1976 to 70,000 in 1981-82 and over 100,000 in 1985-86.[15]

Many of these new entrants have been one-parent families living on supplementary benefits. The percentage of such families in Britain who were in council housing has increased from about half in the mid-1970s to nearly two-thirds in the early 1980s.[16] There is a contrast with the housing of two-parent families; in 1982-83 between a quarter and a third of all such families in Britain were in council housing.[17]

A further dimension is race or ethnic origin. The Labour Force Survey of 1984, covering England, found that the percentage of 'whites' who were in council housing was the same as that in the population generally, 28 per cent. Indians, Pakistanis and Bangladeshis were under-represented, with 15 per cent. West Indians and Guyanese, on the other hand, were over-represented, with 57 per cent in council housing.[18] These figures are broadly in line with those in the Policy Studies Institute 1982 survey of *Black and White Britain*,[19] which covered England and Wales and, by comparing with surveys in 1974 and 1977, was able to examine trends over time. These comparisons showed increases in the proportions of both West Indians and Asians in council housing. Over the eight years from 1974 to 1982, the proportion of West Indians had gone up by over two-thirds and there was a four-fold increase in the proportion of Asians.

The impact of council house sales
A final question for this chapter is about the effect of council house sales on the process of polarisation. Sales to sitting tenants have taken place under Labour as well as Conservative governments from the early 1970s onwards. But the more recent Conservative policy has, through increases in discounts and the like, made purchase easier. Between

1979 and mid-1987 over a million council homes were sold in England and Wales, three times the number sold in the previous 40 years.

Research by Forrest and Murie in England and Wales [20] and by Foulis[21] and Williams, Sewel and Twine[22] in Scotland points to similar conclusions about those who buy. Purchasers are more often in middle life, have non-manual or skilled manual occupations, have relatively high incomes, and are in households with two or more earners. Non-purchasers are more often relatively young or old, are retired or single parents, have unskilled occupations or none, have low incomes, and have no earners or only one in the household.

Regional and local variations reflect these differences. Sales have been highest in the South-East (accounting for over one in three of sales in Britain) and in the Eastern, East Midlands and South-Western Regions. They have been lowest in London, Scotland and the northern Regions. Differences have been even more marked within regions than between them. They have been high in suburban and rural areas, low in the inner cities; high where owner-occupation dominates, low where council housing does; high in estates with houses, low in flatted estates. Although about a third of the council stock is flats, they accounted for only 5 per cent of all sales between 1981 and 1985, and higher discounts under the 1986 Housing Act do not seem to be having much impact.[23]

So, rather than making the tenures more alike, council house sales have in general had the effect of sharpening the differences between them. There is little doubt that, because of sales, the population composition of the council sector as a whole has continued to become even more different from that of owner-occupation than it would otherwise have been.

Conclusion

It is clear that the two main tenures have become more polarised in Britain, and that the process has accelerated in recent years. The scale of change should not be exaggerated. Council housing still contains a mixture of people. But its tenants now include more low-status, unemployed, elderly, lone-parent, black and poor people than other sectors, and more of all these than it did in the past.

The next chapter examines the extent to which a similar process of polarisation has been occurring within the council sector. We leave over until the end of that chapter two questions which apply to both these dimensions - about the causes of the trends, and about how far they are paralleled in France.

References

(1)   Office of Population Censuses and Surveys, *General Household Survey 1979*, London, HMSO, 1981, Table 3.15, p. 44; *General Household Survey 1985,* London, HMSO, 1987, Table 5.9, p. 35.

(2)   C. Hamnett, 'Housing the two nations: socio-tenurial polarisation in England and Wales, 1961-81', *Urban Studies*, 21 (4), 1984, pp.389-400.

(3)   P. Somerville, 'Housing tenure polarisation', *Housing Review*, 35 (6), 1986, pp.190-3.

(4)   Information provided by the Department of the Environment.

(5)   Information provided by the Department of the Environment. The figures for 1962 refer to England, for 1971 and 1978 to Great Britain and for 1982 to England and Wales.

(6)   Information provided by the Department of the Environment. The figures for 1962 refer to England, for 1971 and 1978 to Great Britain and for 1982 to England and Wales.

(7)   Information provided by the Department of the Environment.

(8)   *Hansard,* vol. 108, cols.346-8.

(9)   Calculated from Tables 6.1 (p.45) and 6.8 (p.50) of Office of Population Censuses and Surveys, *Labour Force Survey 1983 and 1984,* London, HMSO, 1986.

(10) Ibid., p.47.

(11) A.E. Holmans, *Housing Policy in Britain*, London, Croom Helm, 1987, p.193.

(12) M. Murphy and O. Sullivan, 'Unemployment, housing and household structure among young adults', *Journal of Social Policy,* 15 (2), 1986, pp.205-22.

(13) Central Statistical Office, *Social Trends,* 17, London, HMSO, 1987, Table 8.5, p.140.

(14) Unpublished analysis by M. Murphy and O. Sullivan, cited in A.E. Holmans, op. cit., p. 212.

(15) Central Statistical Office, *Social Trends, 8* , London, HMSO, 1977, p.155; *Social Trends, 14,* London, HMSO, 1983, p.127; Central Statistical Office, *Social Trends, 18,* London, HMSO, 1988, p.134.

(16) Department of Health and Social Security, *Social Security Statistics,* London, HMSO, 1987, Table 35.59, p.197, and similar tables for earlier years.

(17) Office of Population Censuses and Surveys, *General Household Survey 1983,* London, HMSO, 1985, Table 3.19, p. 20.

(18) Office of Population Censuses and Surveys, *Labour Force Survey 1983 and 1984,* London, HMSO, 1986.

(19) C. Brown, *Black and White Britain,* The Third PSI Survey, London, Policy Studies Institute, 1984, Table 62, p.126.

(20) R. Forrest and A. Murie, *Selling the Welfare State*, London, Croom Helm, forthcoming.

(21) M.B. Foulis, *Council House Sales in Scotland 1979-83,* Edinburgh, Scottish Office Central Research Unit, 1985.

(22) N.J Williams, J. Sewel and F. Twine, 'Council house sales and residualisation', *Journal of Social Policy,* 15 (3), 1986, pp.273-292.

(23) R. Forrest and A. Murie, op. cit.

4 Polarisation Within Social Housing

The changes in the population structure of council tenants in Britain have not been uniform within the sector, any more than they have, as we show later, in social housing in France. The physical standards, population mix and 'image' of British council housing vary by region, by district, by date of construction and by physical form (houses versus flats, high rise versus low rise, systems-built versus conventional construction), and these various dimensions are often inter-related - for example, the mass housing estates of the 1950s and 1960s are mainly located in inner areas. There are manifest differences between that kind of council housing on the one hand and estates in rural and suburban areas on the other.

Council estates which were developed at different dates under different legislation were built to different standards and for different kinds of household. This does not only apply since 1945, where the mass housing contrasts so sharply with what went before and what has come after. For example, the cottage estates built in the interwar years for general needs housing differ from housing built for slum clearance in the 1930s - the former were built to higher standards and the latter were more likely to include flats or houses of experimental design.

Several other changes have affected the physical character of the stock. The acquisition of older houses and the dilapidation of purpose-built dwellings have between them made the sector even more varied than it was half a century ago. The non-traditional high rise point and slab blocks contrast sharply with the earlier four-storey neo-georgian blocks and suburban cottage estates. Reflecting changed objectives, sheltered housing and special needs housing have grown to be sizeable elements in the stock, introducing new kinds of variety into a tenure which previously was mainly for families.

Social changes within council housing

As well as such physical differences within the stock, changes in rents, subsidies, rebates and housing benefit have affected the population mix in different parts of the sector. In some earlier phases since council housing began, and in some localities, the initial rents were high and for a long time tenants were selected on the basis of judgements by housing officers about their ability to pay them. This picture has changed over the last decade or so. Access has become easier for poorer households, and their concentration has grown in areas (especially some mass housing estates and some unpopular older estates) where lettings were available.

The social composition of different parts of the council stock thus now reflects not only when they were first let but also the changing characteristics of those entering the sector at particular phases. Differential movement, both out of council housing and within it, have complicated this process. Relatively affluent people, if they stay in council housing at all, are likely to transfer to houses with gardens, and such moves obviously affect the social composition among those left behind on particular estates.

Family-cycle patterns also have an influence. Estates housing mainly families with children may have high child densities, and this may then discourage people without children from moving in for a decade and a half. Later on, as a result of the relatively low mobility within council housing, what were originally family estates often became estates containing large proportions of elderly people.

Local (sometimes very local) economic circumstances can also play a part. Council estates with heavy dependence on particular industries or employers are affected by redundancies and factory closures. If there is already high unemployment on such estates, it may well become more and more difficult for their residents to find work, because information about job opportunities, and links with firms, may atrophy. By contrast, on estates where a high proportion of the population is in jobs people are more likely to hear of vacancies and to be recommended for them.

The filtering process

It is important to understand the processes which lead to concentrations of disadvantaged people in low-status and usually low-quality estates and dwelling types. Research studies on the subject make it clear that households with low incomes or low bargaining power - which often go together - tend to be housed in the council sector and, within that sector, in the least popular properties.[1]

In talking about unemployed people in the previous chapter we briefly mentioned their tendency to move into council housing. Not only among unemployed people but more generally, and both as between tenures and within council housing, households' differences in resources, opportunities and access are crucial influences upon the kind of housing they get. In terms of tenure, it is obvious that most homes are bought with the help of a mortgage, and that getting a mortgage depends on having a job and an adequate income. With a shrinking private rented sector, people without jobs and adequate incomes are likely to enter council housing. Those who have least hope of getting suitable housing in other tenures are most likely to apply for, and to have to wait for, council housing; this includes homeless families and those affected by slum clearance and improvement policies.

Within council housing the same disadvantaged people are, in the same way, likely to find themselves in the worst dwellings and the worst estates. The internal workings of the public sector tend to channel different kinds of people towards different parts of the stock. Although the allocation procedures are crucial to the process, the detailed arrangements do not matter much in themselves. Whatever the particular local system, councils' practices and rules about matching household size and dwelling size, about the grading of properties, about offers and refusals - all these determine which queue a household is in. Some of these queues require the applicant to wait for a property to become available in a particular estate (because of property size or grading, or sometimes because of the applicant's choice). The ability of applicants to delay and wait for a better offer - their bargaining power within the allocation system - strongly influences which queue they are in and which property they get.

Those with least bargaining power tend to be in the queues for the least desirable properties and tend to be least able to wait for better properties even in such queues. They will usually join the fastest moving queues - those which have the fewest high priority people ahead of them. So, rather than one queue or waiting list operating for council housing in a particular area, there are in reality separate queues or waiting lists - or, as it might be put, different markets - for different parts of the stock. Households with more bargaining power can compete for better housing and those with least bargaining power can compete only for the housing in least demand. Queues move at different speeds, with the queues for the most desirable and scarcest homes being the slowest to progress. Those desperate for rapid rehousing have little chance unless they join the fastest queues and accept the property offered.

Another set of influences, as shown in the recently published study of Birmingham's allocations in the late 1970s,[2] concern the pressures on council officers when they come to allocate tenants to particular estates. Two of their main tasks are to let dwellings as quickly as possible, and to avoid management problems - those that might arise, for example, from mixing 'rough' people with 'respectable' ones. Both these objectives lead them to allocate housing in ways that make for the easiest 'fit', based on the officers' judgements about which kinds of people are likely to be most appropriate for particular estates. They seek to match the people to the dwellings and estates which they think will best 'suit' them. The study suggests that, almost irrespective of the values of particular officers and of the detailed local arrangements, the system is likely to encourage segregation. To put it simply, the understandable desire to ease the problems of lettings and management makes for social segregation among council tenants.

The consequence of all this is that low-income people, and those disadvantaged in other ways, are concentrated in low-quality housing on low-quality estates. The process, once started, is further encouraged by movement out, through transfers or house purchase, on the part of those residents who can go elsewhere. To some extent tenants themselves, particularly the better-off ones, 'vote with their feet' for segregation.

So the operations of the public sector have built into them mechanisms which select and segregate people according to their resources, including income, and their bargaining power. These are the processes which lie behind polarisation - or social segregation - within council housing.

Evidence of the consequences

A number of research studies show the results of the processes we have described. Clapham and Kintrea examined, for example, the relationship between the income per head of household and the popularity of council housing in part of Glasgow.[3] They found that:

> Although only 30 per cent of all households have *per capita* incomes of £18.00 a week or less, 55 per cent of those who accept a house in the least popular group of sub-areas fall into this category. Similarly, at the other end of the income scale, 16 per cent of households have per capita incomes of £52.50 a week or more, but 27 per cent of those in the most popular group of sub-areas have such an income. This makes it clear that poorer people are being allocated less popular housing than better-off people.

Much of the relevant research has concentrated on the relationship between race and housing, and there is more evidence about that than about other influences. Several surveys in the early 1970s showed that blacks were more often in the worst parts of the council stock.[4] Brown's report of the most recent PSI survey (in 1982) confirmed these findings:

> ... blacks are found in flats far more commonly than the rest of the population, their flats are located more frequently on the upper floors, and the relatively small proportion of council houses allocated to black tenants tend to be the less desirable properties ... over a third of black tenants live in flats with entrances above ground-floor level, twice the proportion found among whites. Despite the fact that black tenants are disproportionately located in blocks of flats, they also have a

larger than average share of property built before the first world war ... The properties allocated to black tenants (taking houses and flats together) are smaller than those allocated to white tenants by an average of half a room ... this means there are considerably more black households with high densities of persons per room.[5]

Comparing the 1982 survey with that done by PSI in 1974, Brown reported that polarisation by skin colour had in some respects accelerated:

The disparity between the dwelling types allocated to white and black tenants actually grew in this period: there are now proportionately fewer black tenants in houses, especially detached and semi-detached houses, than in the mid-70s.

Other research in particular towns and cities shows similar patterns. A study in Nottingham found:

West Indians come into the housing system in far greater proportions than whites or Asians (42 per cent, 30 per cent and 16 per cent respectively) through the low-priority gateway of the waiting lists ... The disadvantage and inequalities created by this pattern were then compounded by the extent to which blacks failed to obtain transfers at anything like the same rate as whites ... In terms of the moves which did take place the majority of West Indian rehousing was to postwar council built estates. However, some 80 per cent of these moves were to deck-access or multi-storey flats complexes. These complexes were (and are) amongst the least popular and most stigmatised parts of the council housing stock.[6]

A study of Liverpool carried out by the Commission for Racial Equality in 1984 described the residential concentration of black people in that city. Over a third of black households in Liverpool were in council housing, and access to and allocation of council housing had an important impact on the quality of black people's housing and on their spatial concentration. As black people were concentrated in the housing district which had 83 per cent flats compared to a city average of 50 per cent, the geographical concentration also meant concentration in flats. The study concluded that black households generally received poorer quality accommodation than whites, and the researchers identified their low bargaining power and the stereotyped perceptions of black applicants by housing officials as among the causes.[7]

Research in Tower Hamlets in 1984 found that a larger proportion (39 per cent) of Asian residents than of people in other groups were classified as homeless and therefore graded for less desirable properties.[8] The different range of estates offered to Asians and non-Asians was in part a reflection of where people said they wanted to live, the Asians' choices being influenced by the pull of ethnic community facilities, the existing concentrations of fellow-Asians resulting from past council allocation policies and practices, the fear of harassment if they went to white estates and even, it seemed, the ways in which information about alternatives had been presented to applicants and then recorded for matching purposes.

It was, however, also clear that Asian and non-Asian applicants who did not express area preferences also received a different range of offers. In these cases judgements must have been made about their respective suitability for particular vacancies on the basis of assumptions about group preferences. The reasons for this discretionary matching derived, at least in part, from management pressures to fill vacancies quickly, and they reflected what was seen as a difficulty in managing multi-racial estates in hostile white areas. They also seemed to reflect some assessment of applicants' worth and the types of offer they deserved. In any event, the effect of the allocation process was to direct Asians towards older estates in one part of Tower Hamlets and non-Asians towards some of the new and popular (mainly white) estates.

Henderson and Karn's Birmingham study tells a similar story, bearing out some of the points made earlier about the pressures on officers to match households to estates:

> The strong preference of whites for the suburbs produced a tendency for inner city vacancies to be offered to West Indians or Asians because housing officers expected white applicants to reject such property.

The authors went on to say:

West Indians and Asians were less satisfied with the properties allocated to them and ... this satisfaction related to the condition of the property. It is therefore invalid to argue that the lower standards of property they received arose from lower expectations.[9]

These various pieces of research give a clear picture in which, for a variety of reasons, non-white residents - like households who had low incomes or were disadvantaged in other ways - were concentrated into the worst properties and the worst estates.

Council house sales and segregation

The impact of council house sales on polarisation within council housing has been greater in some parts of the country, and in some estates, than others. In Aberdeen, as Williams and his colleagues point out,[10] sales have been slow, and the effect on the social characteristics of tenants there relatively small. A number of studies[11] have shown that purchases by sitting tenants have been greatest in the parts of the country where home ownership was already high - in the shires and in the South East outside London. As noted earlier, sales have been higher in the most attractive and sought-after estates - those in suburban rather than in inner areas, those containing houses rather than flats, and those built by traditional rather than 'systems' methods. Where sales have led to more of a mixture of tenures on particular estates, greater polarisation between tenures has not led to greater segregation. But, because sales have varied so widely between districts and estates, most of the worst council estates still contain few home-owners or none, and still contain concentrations of disadvantaged people.

Thus in general council house sales have so far worked to reinforce polarisation within council housing. The concentrations are likely to become even greater on some of the estates where tenants are unable, or reluctant, to buy, as better-off tenants move away from such estates and are replaced by homeless families or newcomers without jobs.

Explanations for the trends

We now have to bring together the threads from both this chapter and the previous one. As well as summing up the conclusions, we look at the explanations for the changes in population structure within social housing and between tenures.

In Britain today some poor people live in privately rented or owner-occupied housing but, as is shown by the evidence we have presented, such people are increasingly concentrated in council housing. The figures available over a reasonably long period indicate that the changes in population structure have been going on for several decades. Though the comparisons do not all show identical patterns of change, they suggest that in some respects the trends may even have been more marked in an earlier period, say the late 1960s, than they were in the 1970s. The changes certainly cannot be laid wholly at the door of the Conservative governments in office since 1979, although the social and economic changes under those governments, as well as their housing policies, have intensified the trends.

The causes of the trends lie in fundamental social and economic currents, as well as in what has been happening to housing in Britain, generally and within social housing itself. The wider changes include the economic recession and the subsequent upheavals in Britain's industrial structure, which have left a sizeable minority of the population unemployed or under-employed and wholly or largely dependent on welfare benefits. Various studies have shown the widening gap in living standards between these people and the rest of the population,[12] and the changes in housing reflect this development.

The disadvantaged minority is made up of various groups of people whose numbers have increased. As well as unemployed people, they include divorced and separated people, single parents and retired people. There are more of the latter than there were because of the recession and also because of the changing age structure of the population. As the numbers of retired and early retired people have increased in the general population, they have increased disproportionately in council housing; this is partly because the people who were parents with young children in the period of greatest postwar growth in council housing are now in their 60s and 70s, and partly because that is the sector in which pensioners can most readily afford to live or, to put it the other way, can least readily leave for one of the other options. Other social changes include the increasing propensity of elderly people and in particular widows and widowers to live alone;

given that many of them have low incomes, they are again more likely to be in council housing than elsewhere.

These points are related to the changes within housing markets. As we have shown, disadvantaged people are concentrated in council housing rather than another tenure because of the decline in private renting and the growth in owner-occupation, together with other trends which have made council housing an increasingly unattractive sector, encouraging those who could afford to move out to do so. Changes over recent decades in the balance of ages, types and physical conditions of the council stock have made the sector as a whole less and less desirable to residents in comparison with owner-occupation. It has increasingly ceased to be a sector of high standard, well-equipped and 'modern' housing. It now contains a smaller proportion of attractive homes than it used to and a proportion much smaller than owner-occupation currently contains; in particular (following council house sales) it has proportionately fewer houses with gardens than it did in the late 1950s or early 1960s. These developments, together with what is seen as a 'social' decline among tenants, have encouraged the movement out of some people who might have stayed but could choose not to.

The concurrent changes in the other two sectors have had an even greater influence. The collapse of private renting has removed the main other sector which in the past has housed poor and disadvantaged people. Meanwhile, the financial and other measures introduced by both Labour and Conservative governments to encourage owner-occupation have had serious consequences. They have further reduced the stock of private rented properties, pushed up house prices and drawn off, from private and council renting alike, more and more households for whom house purchase became feasible. These include the former sitting tenants who have been helped to buy their council homes. Alongside the 'push' factor - the apparent physical and social deterioration of public housing - there has been the 'pull' of owner-occupation, with all its financial and other attractions.

Partly in response to such trends as these in the other two housing sectors, the objectives of official policy since the 1969 Cullingworth Report on *Council Housing: Purposes, Procedures and Priorities,*[13] have included widening access to council housing by low-income and ethnic minority households who had previously often been excluded by local allocation policies and by high local authority rents. The process has continued with the priority given in the homelessness legislation, already mentioned, to families with children and others.

The decline of private renting and the encouragement to home ownership made it virtually inevitable that this would happen - that governments would look to councils to house those excluded from the other two sectors. The process of polarisation between tenures is the logical consequence of policies which, emphasis apart, have been bipartisan over the last two decades. The more that access to owner-occupation is extended, the more it is bound to pull in households just at the margin of being able to afford it. Increasingly that leaves behind a relatively pauperised group, those people who cannot afford to make the move. Polarisation as between the population living in council housing and that in owner-occupation should surprise nobody. It was bound to happen, and - on present policies - is bound to continue.

Polarisation *within* council housing also seems certain to continue. The concentration of poor people in the worst council dwellings and estates results from the processes we have described in this chapter. The most disadvantaged people are bound to be the most vulnerable, to have the weakest bargaining power. The resulting polarisation can only be reversed if the standards on the worst estates begin to match those on the best - something that will be very difficult to achieve. Various initiatives, including the government's Priority Estates Project, are doing something to improve unpopular estates, but the social, economic and external housing pressures are so powerful that it would be over-sanguine to expect such small-scale refurbishment programmes and changes in local management to have much impact by themselves.

The obvious question is how much all this matters. We have said that polarisation is inevitable, and it will be bound to continue to some extent occur even if policies are changed. As Donnison has put it, 'Years ago, we used to criticise the councils for failing to house the poorest people: should we grumble now that they have achieved what we asked for?'[14]

As we have said, councils are bound increasingly to house the poorest sections of the population, and we should of course welcome this change. The main concerns are that social housing may become predominantly welfare housing - housing for poor people only - and that the most disadvantaged of all are increasingly concentrated in the worst estates. The housing on such estates - in terms of the dwellings themselves, the estate and its surroundings - is far below the standard enjoyed by the rest of the population. As well as the poor physical conditions, the social environment can be hostile and frightening: such estates are often dangerously insecure. Conditions like these should surely not be considered acceptable in a civilised society.

A second important reason for reversing the current trends is the effect of stigma. Polarisation is socially divisive, often marking people off from the rest of society. This applies again particularly to the residents of the worst estates, whose opportunities suffer. On top of being poor and living in bad housing, they are disadvantaged in other ways - in education, in looking for work, in their dealings with officialdom. To the extent to which the least fortunate are concentrated in the most notorious estates, they are stamped by others with the stigma of failure, and are condemned to suffer in consequence. As council housing becomes more and more a form of segregated housing - or 'ghetto' or 'welfare' housing - the same thing is likely to apply to a growing proportion of council tenants in Britain. Efforts to improve the physical and management standards of the worst housing, though helpful, are unlikely by themselves to be enough to offset these other developments. A more fundamental attack on polarisation is needed.

Trends in polarisation in France
The last question for this chapter is how far there have been similar trends in France to those in Britain, again both within social housing and between tenures.

The 1982 census in France showed that at that date certain sorts of people were more heavily represented in HLMs than in other kinds of housing. For example, 41 per cent of households in HLMs were headed by a manual worker, compared with 25 per cent of all households in France; 9 per cent of HLM households were one-parent families, compared with 4 per cent in France as a whole; 12 per cent of HLM households, as against 7 per cent in France, were made up of couples with three or more children.[15]

A recent article in the monthly journal of the official *Institut National de la Statistique et des Études Économiques* showed a continuing trend in terms of income.[16] The proportion of households whose income was below the national median rose from 48 per cent in 1978 to 59 per cent in 1984. Among households who had moved into an HLM between 1981 and 1984 the proportion was 62 per cent. The same article reported that the proportion of HLM tenants receiving housing benefit had risen from 36 per cent in 1978 to 42 per cent in 1984, and was 47 per cent among those who had recently moved in.

It is clear that polarisation has particularly affected the *grands ensembles*. As a recent article put it:

> The majority of *grands ensembles*... (house) an essentially working-class population. In these areas there is often a high incidence of low wage-earners, unemployment, large families, one-parent families, people with a low level of educational attainment and immigrants, particularly of North African origin ... *Grands ensembles* have come to house a disproportionate number of disadvantaged people.[17]

The commission set up by the French government (*La Commission Nationale pour le Développement Social des Quartiers* or the National Commission for the Social Development of Neighbourhoods) said:

> Under-educated, under-qualified, the inhabitants of the *grands ensembles* are the first to be named when redundancies are announced by a local firm. The level of unemployment is often 30 per cent of the economically active, and in addition more than half of the school-leavers are unable to find a job ... Forty per cent of all immigrants, compared with 20 per cent of all French families, live in the HLMs. In some estates the proportion of foreigners is as high as 30 per cent.[18]

Some of the forms of polarisation in French social housing are different from those noted in Britain. Larger than average proportions of young people are reported, for instance; people aged under 20 account for 30 per cent of the population of France but 50 per cent of that of the *grands ensembles*. This is presumably partly because more of the stock has been built since the 1950s. But, in terms of social status and poverty - as measured by occupation, education, unemployment, single-parent households and low income - the picture is much the same as in Britain. Polarisation has been occurring between social housing and owner-occupation and between the *grands ensembles* and other HLMs.

The main explanations are also the same. In France as in Britain, most people would prefer to buy rather than rent. As in Britain, official policy has been to support the extension of owner-occupation. In consequence:

> During the 1970s the more comfortably-off categories left (the *grands ensembles)* for other housing, in particular for houses of their own. The homes they vacated were relet to immigrant families or to households from the worst slums.[19]

Despite the differences between the two systems, the processes are apparently similar: a 'push' out of social housing because of its social and physical decline has been accompanied by a 'pull' into home ownership, helped by generous government support. In France as in Britain, social polarisation seems to be an inevitable process unless governments take deliberate measures to reverse it. What they are doing, and what they might do, are discussed later.

References

(1) The evidence is summarised in P. Malpass and A. Murie, *Housing Policy and Practice,* Second edition, London, Macmillan, 1987, pp.248-69.

(2) J. Henderson and V. Karn, *Race, Class and State Housing,* Aldershot, Gower, 1987.

(3) D. Clapham and K. Kintrea, 'Rationing, choice and constraint: the allocation of public housing in Glasgow', *Journal of Social Policy,* 15 (1), 1986, pp.51-67.

(4) See for example N. McIntosh and D.J. Smith, *Racial Minorities and Public Housing,* London, Political and Economic Planning, 1975.

(5) C. Brown, *Black and White Britain,* The Third PSI Survey, London, Heinemann, 1984.

(6) A. Simpson, *Stacking the Decks,* Nottingham, Nottingham and District Council for Racial Equality, 1981.

(7) Council for Racial Equality, *Race and Housing in Liverpool: a Research Report*, Liverpool, Council for Racial Equality, 1984.

(8) D. Phillips, *What Price Equality?*, London, Greater London Council, 1985.

(9) Henderson and Karn, op. cit.

(10) N.J Williams, J. Sewel and F. Twine, 'Council house sales and residualisation', *Journal of Social Policy*, 15 (3), 1986, pp.273-292.

(11) R. Forrest and A. Murie, *Selling the Welfare State*, London, Croom Helm, forthcoming.

(12) See for example J. Mack and S. Lansley, *Poor Britain,* London, Allen and Unwin, 1985; P. Townsend, with P. Corrigan and U. Kowarzik, *Poverty and Labour in London,* London, Low Pay Unit, 1987; A.H. Halsey 'Social trends since World War Two', *Social Trends,* 17, London, HMSO, 1987, pp. 11-19.

(13) Cullingworth Report, *Council Housing: Purposes, Procedures and Priorities*, London, HMSO, 1969.

(14) D. Donnison, *The Housing Service of the Future,* Faculty of Scoial Sciences and Arts Lecture, Salford, University of Salford, 1986.

(15) J. Robert, 'HLM, quelles clientèles?', *Aspects Economiques de l'Ile de France*, 19, 1987.

(16) G. Curci, 'Les HLM: une vocation sociale qui s'accentue', *Economie et Statistique*, 26, January 1988, pp.45-55.

(17) J.N. Tuppen and P. Mingret, 'Suburban malaise in French cities: the quest for a solution', *Town Planning Review*, 57 (2), 1986, pp.187-201.

(18) Commission Nationale Pour le Développement Social des Quartiers, *Ces Quartiers où s'Invente la Ville*, Paris, Commission Nationale Pour le Développement Social des Quartiers, 1985, p.7.

(19) N. Haumont, 'Sociologie des grands ensembles', in *Encyclopaedia Universalis*, Paris, 1983.

5 The Management and Maintenance of Social Housing

Polarisation is bound up - as cause or effect - with most of the other problems afflicting council housing in Britain. This chapter is about some of those other problems.

A number of reports give a general picture of what the difficulties are. One of the most authoritative is a 1986 report by the Audit Commission, based on an examination of the 401 local housing authorities in England and Wales. The Commission reported that 85 per cent of council-owned dwellings needed repairs and improvements, with a backlog costing around £20 billion, and with the physical condition of the council stock getting steadily worse. Meanwhile, councils' waiting lists were lengthening and the numbers of homeless households growing. There were 110,000 empty properties, of which 26,000 had been vacant for more than a year. And the Commission expressed concern at the standard of housing management in a number of authorities 'where money is being spent on a growing bureaucracy, rather than on better services for tenants'.[1]

Other studies have focussed on the worst - and the least popular - estates. A Department of the Environment report, in 1980, found that unpopularity - reflected in high rates of vacancy, turnover or transfer applications on particular estates - went with the location, design and density of the estates, with remote and overstretched management, with inadequate maintenance, limited communal facilities and wider social processes. The report commented:

These factors tend to combine so that, as the estates acquire a bad name, the better off families move out and their place is filled increasingly by families with social problems of one sort or another ... the estates tend to get caught in a downward spiral which is difficult to break; poor maintenance, vandalism and high tenant turnover affect the morale and confidence of the residents who all too often feel that their situation is desperate and beyond change.[2]

The government's Priority Estates Project (PEP), which was itself started in an attempt to deal with the problems of such estates, carried out research on 20 of the worst of them, which then became the subject of special attention. The report of the initial PEP study highlighted 'neglected rubbish-strewn environment', 'poor repairs and maintenance' and 'high levels of crime and vandalism', together with higher than average proportions of tenants who were unemployed or living on supplementary benefit. Problems of high turnover, rent arrears, high child densities, empty properties, structural defects, poor location and 'unsuitable design' were also identifed.[3]

Against this background, we look at four current problems of British council housing - rent arrears, empty properties, allocation and maintenance.

Rent arrears

The statistics show that rent arrears in the council sector have been rising, and they are commonly thought to be dangerously high and out of control. They are certainly much higher than mortgage arrears, although these have increased dramatically in recent years.

Duncan and Kirby[4] studied rent arrears in England and Wales between 1972-73 and 1981-82. They found that, as a percentage of the total collectable rent, arrears increased from 1.8 per cent to 4.4 per cent. The Audit Commission, which examined arrears in a special study, looked at changes between 1981 and 1983.[5] Though the Commission did not present comparable figures to those of Duncan and Kirby, it concluded that 'The trend in rent arrears is ... disturbing ... arrears have risen dramatically in the last two years'. It noted, incidentally, that there had been sharp increases in arrears in housing associations as well as council housing. The two studies thus showed a clear trend over time.

Several points of qualification need to be added. The first is that the later and more general Audit Commission report, which included some more up-to-date evidence, found that, though arrears had continued to rise in some local authorities, they had stabilised or fallen in others. Secondly, local authorities are, in comparison with other creditors, less willing to write off past debts, so that in one sense the accumulated figures give a worse impression than is justified, particularly in comparison with other kinds of debt. The Audit Commission said that the level of write-offs was 'unreasonably low', and Duncan and Kirby that 'Gross rent arrears figures need to be approximately halved to give a realistic estimate of the arrears of current tenants seriously behind with their rent'. Thirdly, though the total debt had increased, the proportion of tenants in arrears did not seem to have risen; it was reported to be a quarter in both studies. Fourthly, Duncan and Kirby found that, of the tenants who were in debt, only about a quarter were 'in serious arrears'; the others were in debt because of 'late payment' or 'administrative factors'. The Audit Commission reports did not give more recent figures on this.

The problem is, nevertheless, a serious one. As suggested earlier, it is concentrated in particular kinds of place. Duncan and Kirby reported that arrears were higher in metropolitan districts and London boroughs than elsewhere, and particularly in 'deprived inner urban areas'. The Audit Commission found the same: in 1983 the inner London boroughs, which accounted for one in 20 of all of the public housing tenants in England and Wales, carried just over a quarter of the total arrears, and by the time of the second Commission report the gap had been widening - the authorities with the biggest arrears in 1983 had even bigger arrears in 1984.

At least part of the explanation is that such places contained concentrations of poor people. Duncan and Kirby showed that households with serious rent arrears were usually caught up in a 'complex web of financial difficulties characterised by low income, sudden drops in income or increased demands on the family budget'. The households concerned were mainly families with children, particularly those with three or more, or were single-parent families. The Audit Commission, not surprisingly, likewise found unemployment to be one of the main causes of arrears.

The proportions of unemployed people, households with low incomes, single-parent families and the like have of course increased in the last decade, and have increased disproportionately in social housing. Since families are rarely evicted, those with very low incomes are tempted to give higher priority to spending on such items as fuel, light and food than on rent. In a period when there are more poor people and when more of them have been concentrated into one housing sector, the increase in rent arrears in that sector was almost inevitable.

Unemployment and poverty are, however, not the only explanations for the recent increase in arrears. The Audit Commission noted that the introduction of the relatively new system of housing benefit had caused problems, along with general administrative strains on local authority housing departments. It also concluded that councils varied in the efficiency with which they handled rents. Drawing attention to the contrasts, even in inner London, with other boroughs potentially facing the same problems, it showed that some councils managed things better: they were more effective at avoiding arrears and they dealt more expeditiously with those they did have.

There are thus three conclusions about arrears. First, the problem, though worrying, has been presented as somewhat more serious than it is. It would be sensible for local authorities to follow the practice of other creditors and write off debts that are unlikely to be recovered, especially those of former tenants. Secondly, at least to some extent the money problems which are expressed in high levels of arrears are the result of the economic recession and of demographic and social changes, and they arise in social housing because of the process of polarisation, which has meant that its tenants are more likely than those in other tenures to be poor and vulnerable. But thirdly, the Audit Commission is right to suggest that the case of rent arrears also points up a management problem which needs to be tackled.

Empty properties

One of the most persistent complaints levelled at local authority housing management is about the numbers of empty properties. In recent years government ministers have regularly argued that, rather than relying on new investment, councils could reduce housing needs if they had many fewer empty properties. The Audit Commission's 1986 report referred to the number of council owned dwellings vacant at the end of March 1984. The proportion was 2.4 per cent of the total stock. Councils' Housing Investment Programme returns for 1986 suggested a 2.5 per cent vacancy rate for local authority housing.

Over three-quarters of vacant council dwellings are not actually available for letting; they are undergoing or awaiting repair, improvement, sale or demolition. As the Audit Commission commented, the general level of empty council dwellings compares favourably with other sectors of the housing market. At the same time it argues that those councils with much higher than average levels of empty property could reasonably be expected to reduce the numbers.

This is a sensible and balanced assessment. Empty property is not always a sign of poor management, and a frictional level of vacancies is an indication of inevitable, and proper, mobility and turnover. Even where the level of empty property is high, there may be a number of reasons other than poor management - a lack of funds for investment, the short planning cycle associated with control of housing investment, or the subsidy and cost control system. The main determinant of the speed at which empty dwellings are relet is, however, the management of repairs and allocations. Apart from this, an effective way of reducing the number of empty properties would be to cut the time it takes to relet properties. But it is not at all clear that there is any better model for doing this than the best practice *within* council housing. No doubt there is room for improvement, especially in the time some councils take to carry out redecorations and repairs, but it would be wrong to suggest that in general councils have a bad record in this respect.

Indeed it may be that the consequences of achieving low rates of vacancy in some areas should attract at least as much attention as the relatively high rates in others. Partly because of the anxiety about having empty dwellings, and partly because of an understandable desire to maximise rent income, there has been strong pressure on housing managers and on allocation procedures in the council sector to minimise vacancies. This pressure plays a part in the processes described in the previous chapter; the drive to avoid vacancies and fill dwellings can lead housing managers and allocaters to press too hard for a quick match between applicants and properties, and as a result contribute to the concentration of particular kinds of applicant in particular types of dwelling and estate.

Allocation

Estimates of the number of households on local authority waiting lists in England and Wales have fluctuated around the 1.3 million figure for 1986. A recent study tried to measure changes over time and as between areas, taking into account changes in eligibity rules and the effects of inadequate updating procedures. It concluded that, in total, waiting lists had increased over the previous five years. There had, however, been a decline in waiting lists in urban areas and an increase in rural areas and growth areas, and also a decline in the North and an increase in the Midlands and the South.[6]

The methods by which councils manage their waiting lists and seek fair and efficient allocation are, as just suggested, linked to the ways in which they manage their vacancies. We have mentioned the concern on the part of council officers to minimise the period between lets and to avoid allocations which are likely to create management problems. So it is clear that managers' judgements about appropriate allocations do not in practice reflect only formal policy on needs and priorities. They also reflect worries about possible disruption on estates and about transfer requests that might be generated as a result. In this way, as we have suggested, a preoccupation with minimising vacancies may strengthen the tendency to categorise applicants and may thus contribute to polarised allocations.

Similarly, if an 'efficient' management of the waiting list and allocation process is equated with low vacancy rates and is not tempered by considerations of tenant choice, there is a strong pressure to adopt procedures which limit refusals by explicitly denying choice (for example, policies which give homeless families only one offer) or by allocating people according to stereotyped views about where they would best 'fit'. A 'fast and efficient management' of allocations may be achieved by adopting practices which lead to increased segregation - increased polarisation - within the council stock. The bigger the demand for council housing and the more limited the supply, the more this is likely to happen.

Maintenance

Council housing faces an urgent problem of putting its existing stock into good physical order. It has to be said at the outset that, in terms of 'fitness' as that is strictly defined, the sector as a whole has fewer 'unfit' dwellings than either owner-occupied or privately rented property, and it scores better overall than those sectors in the possession of basic amenities - bathrooms, indoor WCs, hot water and the like. At the same time, as the Audit Commission pointed out, the great majority of council homes need some attention - maintenance, updating or both - and these problems are at their worst in certain types of dwelling and certain kinds of estate.

The Department of the Environment's 1985 'inquiry into the condition of the local authority housing stock in England'[7] concluded that over three million council homes, 84 per cent of the total, needed expenditure of £18.84 billion, the average cost per dwelling being nearly £5,000. The total bill for the necessary work was later updated by the Audit Commission to over £20 billion for England and Wales.

As might be expected, the average cost of putting a dwelling into good order is usually higher for older properties. But, as the DOE report put it, 'Generally within each period flats are said (by the local authorities supplying the information) to require more expenditure than houses and non-traditional dwellings more than traditional'. The properties and estates needing substantial attention thus include those in which large proportions of disadvantaged people live.

The figure of £20 billion for repairs and improvements compares with estimated expenditure in 1986-87 of £1,306 million.[8] At the current rate it would thus take 15 years to complete the task, but the problem is worse than that because, on Audit Commission estimates, the backlog is growing at the rate of £900 million a year. It has been calculated that at the current rate of expenditure it will, for example, take councils 21 years to carry out the necessary improvements in heating and insulation. All in all, it seems that, even with higher levels of spending, the volume of required work is likely to grow faster than local authorities can keep up with the deterioration

Councils could obviously do more both to improve their existing stock and to build new homes if they had, or could get access to, the money needed. Their difficulties were spelt out by the Duke of Edinburgh's Inquiry on British housing:

> ... the current regulations mean that local authorities who seek to supply or to improve rented homes are not only fiercely regulated in raising the necessary finance, but are also inhibited from using the capital gains they have realised from the sale of existing housing.[9]

The Audit Commission concluded, perhaps optimistically, that most authorities could manage to do the necessary improvements to their stock 'with the resources available locally' or with 'available private resources'. But it judged that:

> ... in approximately 10 per cent of authorities ... more public expenditure is likely to be needed either in the form of grants or in the form of tax reliefs and housing benefit.

It should be noted that the 10 per cent of authorities in England and Wales referred to own about one million dwellings. This confirms that, even if the Commission is right, the scale of the problem remains immense. More resources will have to be found if the necessary work is to be done.

The pressures on councils

The four examples we have considered of management and maintenance problems in council housing make it clear that there is plenty of room for improvement in the performance of local housing authorities. But the current faults certainly cannot be blamed entirely on poorly run councils. The demands placed on councils are greater than they have ever been in the past. Councils are dealing with a wider range of stock, and some parts of it (notably the mass housing of the 1960s) pose particular problems of repair and maintenance.

The councils' problems have to be looked at against the background of a changing social, economic and political environment. The collapse of private renting, the growth of homelessness, the ageing of the council stock and the changing characteristics of tenants and applicants have coincided with a decline in the supply of council housing because of the dramatic decline in new building and the impact of the Right to Buy policy. Councils have been obliged to sell off their best housing, while being starved of resources to build anew or to maintain their existing stock. The tasks for council housing managers have become much more difficult at the same time as the stock and the available resources have been sharply reduced.

Councils' room to manoeuvre in meeting people's wishes through allocations procedures is directly affected by the reduction in the stock and the increase in demand. And the pressure exerted on managers and allocators as a result of the various changes leads to local decisions which accelerate the processes of polarisation within and between tenures. It has become more difficult to give tenants choice over dwellings and estates, and an increase in external pressures to reduce rent arrears and vacancies can paradoxically make things worse. The various reports on arrears and vacancies offer constructive suggestions, but if the problems of council housing are not addressed in a way which also values choice, mobility and the quality of dwellings, and recognises the current pressures on managers and allocators, the consequences of improvement in one respect may be outweighed elsewhere.

Problems of French social housing

If polarisation has been occurring in France as well as Britain, many of the related issues too are echoed in French social housing. As with polarisation, the problems are concentràted in the *grands ensembles*. But the detailed evidence is sparse.

Such information as is available leaves little doubt that problems are similar. Tuppen and Mingret describe the worst of the *grands ensembles* as constituting:

> ... an environment increasingly characterised by vandalism, crime and violence, leading to a growing sense of insecurity among the population.[10]

The violence has sometimes been extreme. France's riots, in the early 1980s, were in suburban *grands ensembles*, notably *Les Minguettes* at Lyons, others in Marseilles, Nancy and Roubaix, and *Les 4000* at La Courneuve to the north of Paris, rather than in French inner city areas.

Because most French estates were built on the outskirts of cities, they often suffer from problems which are rare in Britain except on some of the larger postwar suburban estates.[11] Suburban HLMs have often been criticised because of the absence of shops, schools, social and sports facilities and public services. Even before the economic recession, the residents of some such estates found that there were few jobs available locally and that the journey to work was long and costly.

The four management issues we have considered in Britain have been causing concern in France as well. For example, rent arrears are reported to have increased. In his comparative report for the OECD, Maclennan noted that HLM rent arrears in general had risen from 3.4 per cent of potential revenue in 1981 to 4.2 per cent in 1984.[12] The levels are broadly comparable to those in British council housing. The problem has been recognised nationally in France as in Britain; in an attempt to reduce arrears through better management, the government and the HLM national union published in December 1986 an 80-page guide for HLM managers entitled *Preventing and Treating Rent Arrears.*[13] A government report on the finances of HLMs echoed the British findings on the causes when it said that there were two main reasons for arrears - the poverty of some tenants and failures on the part of management.[14]

As for vacancies, by 1985 the general level in HLMs was stabilised, at about 3 per cent,[15] again an average level similar to that in British council housing. There have, however, been much higher levels in some of the *grands ensembles*. Les Minguettes, near Lyons, built between 1960 and 1975, had 2,200 dwellings vacant out of a total of 7,500 by 1982. Maclennan said that its vacancy rate:

... varied by location, house size and organisational structure. One HLM, the smallest, had (in 1983) a zero vacancy rate, but eight had rates exceeding 25 per cent ... Within sub-areas the vacancy rate varied from 89 per cent to 14 per cent.[16]

Many HLMs have had to face the familiar problems of trying to find the resources to maintain and modernise their stock, the difficulties being most acute with the *grands ensembles* built in the 1950s and 1960s. The physical conditions on such estates are apparently like those on the worst inner city estates in Britain. Tuppen and Mingret report:

The quality of construction has often been mediocre, leading to problems of ineffective insulation against noise and to the premature decay of buildings. Inadequate and ineffective maintenance has often served to aggravate these shortcomings.[17]

The National Commission for the Social Development of Neighbourhoods said that:

> Leprous-looking facades, degraded staircases, broken shutters, jammed rubbish chutes, open spaces abandoned and of uncertain ownership, swept by the wind, are part of the daily setting for millions of inhabitants.[18]

The majority of the French *grands ensembles* are now over 20 years old, and they urgently need to be refurbished. As in Britain, it is not easy to find the necessary finance to maintain and improve the stock. Maclennan concluded in his report that the costs of rehabilitation and maintenance, when set against income from rents, 'threatens the viability' of the HLMs; 'Throughout France', he commented, 'some 5 per cent of HLMs are now thought to have serious problems and a further 25 per cent face difficulties' [19]

Finally, it is recognised in France, as in Britain, that allocation is important and can generate problems. A criticism of some *office public* HLMs, for instance, is that they, and particularly their mayors, exert too much personal patronage in choosing tenants. At the same time, with both types of HLM a number of other bodies as well as the HLM management itself (and with *offices publics* the municipality and the mayor) can have nomination rights, including local employers and the Prefect. The procedures inevitably affect the population mix, which on particular estates has been a source of social tension. And the various partners have often blamed each other for responsibility for homes being allocated to the 'difficult' elements in the population.

References

(1) Audit Commission, *Managing the Crisis in Council Housing,* London, HMSO, 1986, p.1.

(2) Department of the Environment, *An Investigation of Difficult to let Housing,* Volume 1, General Findings, HDD Occasional Paper 3/80, London, HMSO, 1980.

(3)   A. Power, *Local Housing Management,* Department of the Environment, 1984; see also A. Power, *Property Before People: the Management of Twentieth-Century Council Housing,* London, Allen and Unwin, 1987.

(4)   S. Duncan and K. Kirby, *Preventing Rent Arrears,* London, HMSO, 1983.

(5)   Audit Commission, *Bringing Council Tenants' Arrears Under Control,* HMSO, 1984.

(6)   G. Bramley and D. Paice, *Housing Needs in Non-Metropolitan Areas,* Report of Research for the Association of District Councils, Bristol, University of Bristol, School for Advanced Urban Studies, 1987.

(7)   Department of the Environment, *Inquiry into the Condition of the Local Authority Housing Stock in England*, London, Department of the Environment, 1985.

(8)   Her Majesty's Treasury, *The Government's Expenditure Plans 1987-88 to 1989-90*, Cm. 56-11, London, HMSO, 1987, p. 149.

(9)   Duke of Edinburgh's Inquiry, *Inquiry into British Housing: Report*, London, National Federation of Housing Associations, 1985, p.6.

(10) J.N. Tuppen and P. Mingret, 'Suburban malaise in French cities: the quest for a solution', *Town Planning Review*, 57 (2), 1986, pp.187-201.

(11) The problems of outer estates in Britain are examined in, for example, CES Limited, *Outer Estates in Britain: a 'Framework for Action. Part 1: a Discussion Paper,* CES Paper 28, London, CES Limited, undated; D. Sim, 'Urban deprivation: not just the inner city', *Area,* 16 (4), 1984, pp.299-306.

(12) D. Maclennan, *Maintenance and Modernisation of Urban Housing,* OECD Urban Affairs Programme, Paris, Organisation for Economic Cooperation and Development, 1986, p.50.

(13) *Prévenir et Traiter les Impayés de Loyers*, Paris, Union Nationale des Fédérations d'Organismes d'HLM, 1986.

(14) Direction de la Construction, *Situation Financière des Offices et Sociétés Anonymes d'HLM de 1980 à 1985,* Paris, Ministère de l'Équipment, du Logement, de l'Aménagement de Territoire et des Transports, 1987, p.53.

(15) Ibid., p.25.

(16) Maclennan, op. cit., p.57.

(17) Tuppen and Mingret, op. cit..

(18) Commission Nationale Pour le Développement Social des Quartiers, *Ces Quartiers où s'Invente la Ville,* Paris, Commission Nationale Pour le Développement Social des Quartiers, 1985, p.7.

(19) Maclennan, op. cit., p.58.

6 Learning from French Experience

The similarities in the problems of social housing in the two countries suggest that changes in institutions or detailed policies would in themselves be unlikely to reverse the underlying trends or solve the fundamental problems. Nevertheless, it is still worth asking what ideas France has to offer.

In considering the French experience, there are two main questions. One is whether the HLM institutional form itself is worth emulating in any respects. The other is about specific policies to meet the problems of polarisation and decline described in the previous chapters.

Private renting in France
There is, however, a prior question that deserves some discussion. In comparing tenure patterns in France with those in Britain, a striking feature is that private renting's share is much higher across the Channel - over a quarter compared with under a tenth at the last censuses. Does this suggest that if we followed the French arrangements we could, as the present government wishes, give private renting a much bigger role here?

We examine the prospects for such an expansion in Britain in the next chapter. Here we would say only that the present differences are less a reflection of current policies than of history. Private renting has remained relatively large in France because of the virtual absence of a social housing sector there before 1953, and because of differences over the last 70 years in the extent to which private renting has been subject to controls.

The sector is in any event now contracting in France, and there seem no grounds for believing that it will expand. Our conclusion is that the French experience does not provides any encouragement or guidance to policy makers who seek to develop its role substantially in Britain.

The HLM as a model?

The main argument for the HLM as a form is said to be that it combines the advantages of small scale, single-minded emphasis on housing with independence and accountability. It is suggested that it is able to be more responsive to local needs than a large public body can be, particularly one with a range of other responsibilities, but that it is at the same time subject to public inspection and supervision - properly so, since it receives public funds. These features would seem likely to make it something that the present British government might want to emulate or at least consider. The difficulty is to judge how it works in practice.

In Britain as in France, judgements are coloured by the experience of the unhappiest kind of social housing, the *grands ensembles*. Just as the worst problems of British council housing are characteristic of only part of the stock, so most of French social housing is relatively trouble-free. The *grands ensembles* account for about a third of HLM housing, and not all of them give cause for serious concern. Thousands of small estates - many of them low and medium rise - work relatively successfully in towns and villages all over France. The HLM agencies themselves vary considerably, even within the two main types.

There is certainly official recognition in France that HLMs do not work uniformly well, any more than do local housing authorities in Britain, and that the quality of management in some is poor. The government has launched a campaign, costing 25 million francs (about £2.5 million), to encourage HLMs to bring in experts to help them 'modernise their management'.

Nevertheless, there is no comprehensive body of evidence showing how effectively HLMs are managed, compared either with each other or with British housing authorities. An official report has been published based on analyses of the costs of HLM management,[1] and this shows that in general the finances of *offices publics* HLMs are in better shape than those of *sociétés anonymes*. It suggests that this is partly because they are under more public supervision and because the *sociétés,* conversely, can and do take more risks. The management costs of *offices publics* are shown to be lower, the likely reasons given being that their (public service) salaries are lower and that they achieve some economies because their operations are generally on a larger scale.

The same report shows that, at least in terms of what it calls their 'financial health', the *offices publics* are not only financially sounder in general but are also more homogeneous than the *sociétés anonymes*. About the *sociétés* the report comments: 'while some have relatively brilliant results, the results of others are mediocre, if not catastrophic'.

In the light of this evidence, and following discussions with a number of French experts, we would sum up the differences in performance between the two main kinds of HLM as follows. The *offices publics* are more like each other mainly because they are more subject not only to local authority influence but also to supervision by state bodies. Their management structures, and their staff, work in a more bureaucratic way. In general their activities are more constrained by regulation and supervision than are those of the *sociétés anonymes*. They are also subject to local, often political, influence and this is sometimes harmful. It should also be borne in mind that their management tasks are greater, since they house the great majority of poor and deprived tenants.

The *sociétés anonymes*, for their part, are more flexible and, since they can be choosier about their tenants, have an easier task anyway. More of them are small. In financial terms they perform less well in general; the worst of them are in dire straits financially and presumably worse managed than the worst *offices publics*. These conclusions about the drawbacks of social housing agencies independent of government echo some of the doubts that have been expressed in Britain about substantially expanding the role of housing associations.

An outsider's conclusion about France might be that it would be sensible for it to devise a more independent and flexible form of *office public*, and encourage that. This is precisely what recent government policy has been. A variant on the standard *offices publics*, the OPAC (*offices publics d'aménagement et de construction*), has existed as an option since 1971 but its status was changed and its powers enlarged by a new decree in March 1986. This change is seen as an expression of a general desire to move from bureaucratic forms to new styles of 'entreprise with social objectives'. OPACs are managed by a governing body containing representatives of the local authorities and other public and semi-public bodies, as well as a few representatives elected by tenants. But they have their own finance department (unlike *offices publics*, whose finances are handled by a state *trésor public*); their staff are not public servants; and their extra powers mean that they can operate more freely.

There were still only 27 of them in April 1987, out of 676 HLMs in total. But, having been static in numbers until mid-1986, in one year after the change in their status they increased by 11 from a base of 16. Their numbers and role seem likely to continue to grow.

Although there is no clear evidence whether different types of HLM are better landlords than British local authorities or housing associations, there may be a case for looking more closely at them as options for Britain. When we come later to consider possible new forms of social housing for Britain, the OPAC may well be the best of the French models; while ensuring a degree of public accountability, it avoids bureaucracy on the one hand and excessive risks, sometimes with disastrous consequences, on the other.

The French priority programme

The main French response to the problems of the *grands ensembles* is a combined programme for the physical and social improvement of priority *grands ensembles* estates, directed by the government commission quoted in earlier chapters - the National Commission for the Social Development of Neighbourhoods.

The Commission's programme was preceded by a more limited one which started in 1977. As the title of that programme - *Habitat et vie sociale* - may suggest, it too was concerned with both the physical and social environment, and it gave birth to 50 local projects. But in practice these concentrated mainly on physical renewal, and they came up against problems of securing collaboration between the various agencies. Particularly after the *grands ensembles* riots of the early 1980s, they were seen as inadequate.

In 1981 the government asked the National Commission to examine the *grands ensembles*, reporting direct to the Prime Minister. The Commission first reported in 1983; its proposals were accepted and it was then established as a permanent body, with the task of implementing them. An initial 16 projects were expanded to 23 and then, through the Commission's regional bodies and in discussion with the regional and local authorities, to 150 by the middle of 1987. Not surprisingly, the projects concentrate on the worst of the *grands ensembles*; 90 per cent of the Commission's work is on the estates with *tours* (towers), *barres* (slabs) and *immeubles très dense* (high density blocks).

The objectives of the Commission's programme include some closely similar to those of the British government's Priority Estates Project and its broader programme of Estate Action:

- to improve the physical stock;
- to improve management;
- to improve security.

But the Commission also identified the problems of young people on the estates, and in particular their need for jobs, and it wanted to do something to reduce social conflicts and raise morale. So its schemes included additional aims:

- to improve job opportunities and leisure facilities for young people;
- to provide more social, cultural and educational facilities.[2]

The Commission's programme is implemented through *contrats du plan,* firm commitments initiated through the government's broader National Plan but led by the Regional Councils. In an attempt to ensure commitment and collaboration at all levels, the programme represents firm claims on the budgets of all the relevant central government departments, and draws in not only the regional bodies but also the *départements* and the communes, together with other regional and local agencies including the police. Within this structure, local residents - 'the community' - are given an important role: the Commission's initial report spoke of the need for a strategy to encourage 'the active participation of residents' and this seems to have been implemented.[3]

As well as sharing some of the same aims, the French programme is roughly comparable to PEP and Estate Action in its scale and its cost to central government. The 150 priority schemes in France compare with the 127 Estate Action schemes in Britain at about the same date. The total cost to the French government of its programme has been about £70 million each year (£50 million for physical improvement, £20 million for 'social development'). In 1986-87 the British government contributed £50 million in additional Housing Investment Programme resources to this programme and the sum was increased to £75 million in 1987-88. The two programmes are also alike in their attempts to involve or at least consult local people but, as has already been noted, in other respects the British one is more limited. It lays less emphasis on social development and on jobs. In addition, although the total expenditure and the number of schemes are broadly similar, the scale of the French effort is greater in relation to their stock of social housing, which is only half the size.

It is not easy to make a proper assessment of the French programme. These are early days. Some initial enquiries have, however, been made, and the results seem broadly favourable. For instance, 60 HLMs, covering 85 local projects, returned a self-completion questionnaire asking for their views; though there were some criticisms - that the resources were inadequate, that the procedures were too complicated, that it was difficult to mobilise the enthusiasm of tenants - 78 per cent of the HLMs thought the procedures worked effectively and 61 per cent believed that the image and reputation of their estates had improved.[4] The Commission itself reports that the proportion of vacant flats has been reduced, by as much as 20 per cent in some estates, and that there has been a 10 per cent reduction in crime. In his comparative study for the OECD[5] Maclennan was favourably impressed, on three counts.

First, the organisational structure, which he judged to be 'highly appropriate'. A point to add here is that the French system seems to be more successful than the British in ensuring inter-ministry and inter-agency collaboration; this is partly because until 1986 the Commission reported to the Prime Minister rather than a particular minister, and partly because the Regional Prefect and the *Départmental* Prefect, whose coordinating roles are important, are the representatives of central government and, again, stand outside - or above - ministerial rivalries.

Second, although the Regional Council and even more the *département* have substantial responsibilities for launching and overseeing the programmes, the commune has the key coordinating role at the local level, and Maclennan saw this as an arrangement that also worked well.

Third, he commented on the social development and job creation activities which formed part of the priority programme, giving Les Minguettes, Lyons, as an example:

> ... some local residents received advanced training in social participation skills, so that they could be employed in social development aspects of modernisation. Young unemployed youths (around 30 in total) were attached to the reconstruction programme and trained for 18 months. They have subsequently become part of the construction labour force. The number of local concierges employed has more than doubled and there are plans to develop local repair suppliers. Clearly ... these areas cannot solve their problems by 'taking in their own washing', but they can reduce unemployment.

Of these three observations, the first two refer to organisational forms and are relevant to discussions about the long-term future of British social housing, as well as to programmes of improvement. The third is entirely about running priority schemes to improve estates. It seems likely that improving social facilities and providing local employment within refurbishment schemes can help to raise morale and to generate a 'virtuous circle' of physical and social improvement on the most unpopular estates. Extending the scope of refurbishment schemes in such estates in Britain seems to us an idea worth borrowing from across the Channel. Although in total more has probably been done in Britain to create jobs, mainly through Urban Programme schemes and the like, the distinctive approach in the programme of the French National Commission is through employment projects which are targetted on particular estates.

Housing the poor

As well as the priority programme, there is also the more general government scheme to help support HLM refurbishment. This forms part of what we see as a second strand in current French policy for social housing. It has to be said at the outset that the policy developments are relatively new. They have furthermore not been explicitly presented as a 'package' and are seldom discussed in that way. But in combination they are reducing the proportions of poor people living in social housing and thus changing the role of the HLMs.

The starting point was the official recognition that, along with the residualisation or pauperisation of the population in some of the HLM *grands ensembles,* there was also a physical problem of decline, an increase in the level of rent arrears and an increase, too, in the numbers of empty - and unlettable - flats. As a result the HLMs' incomes were falling, but at the same time refurbishment was urgently needed. With declining income on the one hand and the need for substantial spending on maintenance and improvement on the other, many of the HLMs were in financial crisis.

The government response was to provide additional subsidies to the HLMs to meet part of the cost of physical improvements - a wider programme of improvement as well as the priority scheme just described. An advantage for the HLMs was that as part of the deal - an agreement (*conventionnement*) between the government and the HLM - the tenants in the blocks which were improved would be eligible for the income-related housing benefit described in Chapter 2, *Aide personalisée au logement* or APL. But for their part the HLMs agreeing to the arrangements had to institute a new financial regime. They had to ensure that their books moved into balance once more - and stayed there henceforth. The subsidy thus had to be spent in ways that, while improving and maintaining the physical fabric, would also reverse the cycle of decline: HLMs would need to fix rents at higher levels so as to keep the books in balance. Given the APL, this should not have been too difficult for them.

After 10 years, however, only about a quarter of the HLM stock was covered by the *conventionnement* system, one problem being that the HLMs have had to meet most of the cost of modernisation themselves.

As explained in Chapter 2, from January 1988 the HLM bodies will be able to enter into a new type of *convention sans travaux* (agreement without works being carried out), under which rents can rise to reflect the value of the property and low-income tenants will become eligible for APL2 (at lower than standard APL rates). Some tenants will benefit - those who were not eligible for AL (*Allocation de Logement*) because they were not in one of the special categories. The HLMs will benefit because the APL allowances will (like APL in the past) be paid direct to them, rather than (as the AL has been) to tenants via the *Caisses d'Allocations Familiales*.

The government's support for social housing takes two main forms - it subsidises the cost of borrowing for new building and it subsidises low-income tenants through housing allowances. Each year it has to decide in advance the level of finance which will be available to support loans for new construction of social housing, and to fix the total sum to be set aside for housing allowances.

For the HLM movement the critical point in the discussion each year is when rent levels are fixed. A relatively high level allows modernisation and adequate maintenance but automatically causes an increase in the cost of the APL to the government itself. When the APL was established in 1977, it was believed that the system would be able to strike a workable balance between the level of rents and the level of APL, and up to the beginning of the 1980s this had been more or less achieved in each annual round.

From the early 1980s on, it was clear that the total cost of the APL was rising sharply. This was partly because of what was happening in HLM housing, where more households became eligible for APL as blocks were modernised and their rents increased. It was also because of the steep increase in the number of households buying their homes; if their incomes were low they too were - and are - eligible for APL. The obvious solution would have been to reduce the level of eligibility for APL and thus the total cost, but such a policy would have been politically difficult. The problem for the HLMs was that any reduction in APL support would put more tenants into arrears, upset the financial equilibrium and undermine the modernisation programme.

The problem was examined in two official reports - the Darnault report in 1981[6] and the Laxan report in 1987[7] - but both were more concerned with APL support for home owners than for HLM tenants. The Laxan report did recommend reforming the system of housing benefit for HLM tenants, and as explained earlier the government has accepted this. The financial impact of the change will be a relatively modest increase in the housing benefit bill, building up over three or four years. Meanwhile, in July 1987 as an economy measure the government had slightly reduced the APL scales in real terms. It still faces the underlying problem of striking a balance which avoids too high a bill for APL support while enabling low-income families to afford the (necessarily increased) rents of HLM housing.

An essential element in the HLMs' own financial strategy has been to unburden themselves of their most uneconomic properties. Some blocks have been demolished, like some in Britain. This was done, for example, at La Courneuve, to the north of Paris, at two estates near Lyons and at one south of Roubaix. Other blocks have been left empty. The best known of these is the block designed by Le Corbusier and built in 1961 at Brièy la Forêt, in Lorraine. In 1984 330 of its 339 dwellings were vacant, and it was closed from 1985 on; in 1987 it was taken over by a hospital.

Although the general level of vacant dwellings is relatively low, there are wide variations, as noted in the previous chapter. Les Minguettes, built between 1960 and 1975, had 2,200 dwellings vacant out of a total of 7,500 in 1982. Since then demolition, closures and rehabilitation have eliminated many. At Sillon de Bretagne, near to Nantes, a block of 987 dwellings, constructed in 1965, had a vacancy level of 30 per cent in 1982, subsequently reduced by complete renovation of the block. The HLM buildings that have been demolished or left vacant are the least popular blocks, and these are the ones most likely to have formerly housed large proportions of poor people.

In one way and another, it has become more and more difficult for the HLMs to provide housing for the very poorest tenants. One assumption underlying the 1977 legislation was that the HLMs would from then on house only the *populations solvables* (those who could pay their way) and that this would happen either through tenants themselves having high enough incomes or by them being subsidised through the APL. If the family income is regular but low it can be accepted as an HLM tenant, on the understanding that the government will subsidise its rent through housing allowances. Those who have no regular job or pension are, however, generally excluded from entry to HLMs, and these are in the main the poorest of all. But, apart from moving in with relatives or friends, where are such families expected to live?

A partial official answer has been to try to reduce the costs of housing for low income families by lowering the acceptable standards in constructing or renovating blocks. Until recently government subsidy and housing benefit were available only if the property met minimum standards of space, amenity and so on. After some discussion, there is now official acceptance of *le logement adapté* - dwellings which in space or amenities fall somewhat below those standards.

But the HLMs themselves refuse to take part in official discussions about lowering standards, even in a possible experimental scheme. The idea has, however, been taken up by associations like the *Fédérations des Pacts (Propagande et Action contre les Taudis)*. This federation was set up in 1951 following a number of initiatives by Catholics in Lyon from 1942 onwards and in Lille and Roubaix in the 1950s. A similar group is *La Fédération des Arim (Association pour la Renovation Immobilière)*, which was set up in 1967. These organisations intervene as developers of housing for poor people but outside the HLM framework. Their method is to mobilise public financial support for particularly derelict housing areas, which often means working on housing which falls below the official standards. They provide between 30,000 and 40,000 dwellings a year.

It seems as if the various changes described have had the effect of reducing the numbers of poor tenants in HLM housing. Although, as we showed in Chapter 4, the HLMs have been housing a growing proportion of low-income households, the proportion of very poor tenants has apparently been declining. What PACT and ARIM can do for such people is limited and, though firm evidence is lacking, concern is growing in France over what is seen as a sharp rise in homelessness.

The French government faces an obvious dilemma: in periods when public spending needs to be contained, but support for owner-occupation is felt to be a policy priority, governments seek to reduce or contain the costs to the exchequer of social housing including housing benefits. The problem is evident in Britain, and the government's latest measures, discussed in the next chapter, are intended to meet it, partly by looking more to the private sector while reducing housing benefits. The fear in France is that it will become more and more difficult for the most disadvantaged people to find anywhere decent to live. If that happened, it might be argued that this process reduced social polarisation between owner-occupation and HLM housing. But the housing standards of the poor would be reduced, and their segregation intensified.

Conclusion

Although the limited role of institutional arrangements needs to be borne in mind, it does look as if the French ways of doing things might provide some examples that could be followed in Britain.

The HLM system is clearly not without its own financial and management problems, some at least of which stem, as ours do, from the official priority given to owner-occupation as against renting and from the difficulty of maintaining the stock while restraining public expenditure. But if we in Britain are to be open to new ideas about forms of social housing, then it is worth looking closely - more closely than we have been able to in this report - at the HLM as offering some management models. So far the OPAC form seems the most hopeful one, combining independence and flexibility with accountability for its use of public funds.

Secondly, it looks as if the British priority programme for the worst estates could usefully extend its scope and scale, incorporating some version of the social development and employment elements of the French programme.

A third point is about the respective roles of regional bodies, the *départements* (especially the Prefect) and the municipal authorities in implementing housing policies in France. The French seem to have developed a system, in which the various public authorities below the level of the central government itself have important parts to play - to some extent coordinating, to some extent checking and balancing each other and the individual HLMs. It is an example which might usefully be borne in mind in connection with some of the proposals we offer in the next and final chapter for the organisation of social housing in Britain.

Finally, if French policies are having the effect of reducing the numbers of very poor people in HLMs, this is certainly not an example to emulate. A future policy for social housing in Britain needs to be alert to the same dilemma. Such a policy needs to have two objectives. The first is to ensure that social housing is financially healthy, well-managed and its stock maintained in good order. The second is to provide an adequate supply of decent-standard housing for the poorest families. If in Britain or France social housing is starved of resources it will find it difficult to strike a proper balance between these two aims. This question of housing finance is one of the subjects to which we turn in the next and final chapter.

References

(1)   Direction de la Construction, *Situation Financière des Offices et Sociétés Anonymes d'HLM de 1980 à 1985*, Paris, Ministère de l'Équipment, du Logement, de l'Aménagement de Territoire et des Transports, 1987.

(2)   Commission Nationale Pour le Développement Social des Quartiers, *Ces Quartiers où s'Invente la Ville*, Paris, Commission Nationale Pour le Développement Social des Quartiers, 1985.

(3)   H. Dubedout, *Ensemble, Refaire la Ville*, Rapport au Premier Ministre du Président de la Commission Nationale Pour le Développement Social des Quartiers, Paris, La Documentation Française, 1983, p.35.

(4)   *Les Organismes d'HLM Engagés dans une Procedure de DSQ: Evaluation et Perspectives*, Paris, Union Nationale des Fédérations d'Organismes d'HLM/Commission Nationale Pour le Développement Social des Quartiers, 1987.

(5)   D. Maclennan, *Maintenance and Modernisation of Urban Housing*, OECD Urban Affairs Programme, Paris, Organisation for Economic Cooperation and Development, 1986, p.50.

(6)   Rapport Darnault, *Orientations Pour une Politique Souple d'Accession au Logement*, Rapport au Conseil Économique et Social, Paris, Publication des Journaux Officials, 1987.

(7) Rapport Laxan, *Rapport de la Commission sur les Aides à la Personne en Matière de Logement*, Paris, Union Nationale des Fédérations d'Organismes d'HLM, 1987.

7   The Future of Social Housing

The history of social housing in Britain in recent years is, as earlier chapters have shown, a story of decline. Council housing has become increasingly the sector for poor and disadvantaged people. That is no surprise: with owner-occupation becoming dominant and rented social housing as the main alternative, the latter is bound to contain many more such people than the former. But on present trends the extent of polarisation between the two sectors is a serious cause for concern, for the reasons we gave in Chapter 4. If social housing becomes wholly 'residual' or 'welfare' housing its quality will continue to decline and its inhabitants will become even more stigmatised.

The concentration of disadvantaged people in the worst of the social housing stock is particularly worrying. The problems of maintenance and management, described in Chapter 5, and in particular the continuing physical deterioration of the stock, are no less disturbing. The question for this final chapter is what should be done.

The government's proposals

A starting point must be what the government itself is doing. Its policies have been set out in the 1986 White Paper on housing policy,[1] in the subsequent housing legislation, and in Ministerial statements. The aims are described as providing more rented housing and more choice for tenants. The main proposals are:

- No controls on the rents of new lettings by private landlords or housing associations.

- Council tenants to have the right - Tenants' Choice - to transfer to housing associations, cooperatives or private landlords.
- Government grants to housing associations to be reduced, so as to encourage associations to draw in more private capital.
- Housing Action Trusts (HATs) to take over council housing in selected inner city areas, selling it after renovation to housing associations, cooperatives, trusts or private landlords, or back to the local authority.
- Local authorities to be discouraged from building any more new housing for rent and to own and manage substantially less property than at present, but to play a strategic housing role.

The impact of these housing proposals will be affected by some other government actions. The main ones are changes in the social security system and in housing benefits, and the introduction of the Community Charge or poll tax. These measures are bound to reduce the incomes of at least some low-income families, while the changes in housing policy will result in higher rents in both privately rented and housing association housing.

This combination of proposals has two dangers. The first is that some poorer people, worse off than they have been because of the social security changes and perhaps unable to qualify for housing benefit because of what are judged to be 'excessive rents', may as a result be further concentrated into the worst of the social housing stock. The government's measures would have the effect of further accelerating polarisation. The second danger is that, as has been suggested is happening in France, the poorest people might find it increasingly difficult to stay in social housing at all. These two anxieties need to be taken into account in judging the government's housing policies.

The demand for rented housing

In considering how effective the government's policies are likely to be in dealing with the current problems, key questions are how far there is at present an unmet demand for rented homes, and how far private renting is likely to meet that demand.

Three measures demonstrate the demand for rented housing. First, local authority returns for their Housing Investment Programmes show that in England in 1986 1.3 million households were registered on council waiting lists. It is sometimes suggested that waiting list figures exaggerate the scale of need, but a careful survey carried out for the Association of District Councils on the 1986 figures showed that, even when allowance was made for differences in council procedures, the total figure was unlikely to be far short of the 1.3 million.[2] Secondly, the number of households accepted as homeless increases each year; in Britain in 1986 the figure was 120,000. Thirdly, at the end of 1986 9,000 households in Britain were living in bed and breakfast accommodation and a further 13,000 in hostels and other temporary accommodation.

The Audit Commission said about the consequences of the shortage of rented housing:

> If (for example) a newly married couple cannot afford - or do not want - a commercial mortgage they have little alternative to seeking a council house, since the private sector has contracted in the last two decades. Since 1960 the number of homes available for rent from private landlords has fallen by some 2.5 million, well in excess of the waiting list for council houses or the current housing shortfall[3].

The case for more rented housing is overwhelming, particularly in some parts of the country. Apart from homeless families and others with children, those needing rented housing include elderly people, many of them currently owner-occupiers; in 1987 owner-occupiers accounted for as many as a fifth of all those on council waiting lists, and the proportion was rising. Rented housing is also needed to facilitate movement. The present inadequacy of rented property means, among other things, that unemployed people and people with skills in demand elsewhere in the country are unable to move to the places where there are jobs for them.

The future of private renting
The government's main hope is to increase the supply of rented housing in what it describes as the 'independent' sector, that is housing rented from private landlords, but also from housing associations and

cooperatives. We can understand the reason for this choice of terminology. But, as we explained in the Introduction, in our judgement the distinction between rented housing which is for profit (private) and not for profit (social) is important, and we think the government's alternative split is misleading.

One government aim is 'to encourage new investment' in private renting by enabling landlords 'to charge rents on new lettings at a level that will give them a reasonable return'. The first question is whether the rents that people in sufficient numbers would be prepared to pay would be high enough to attract substantial new investment.

The fullest study so far into the prospects for private renting is the recent one by Whitehead and Kleinman.[4] They concluded that 'even to keep supply up to existing levels would require rents well above current market determined levels'. Landlords would be looking for a level of return comparable to what they could get from other forms of investment and then, given the past history of controls over rents, for something extra by way of compensation for political uncertainty. Potential investors would be inhibited by what Whitehead and Kleinman describe as 'the fear that any change of government would result in the reintroduction of controls'. The financial institutions need to be assured of stable arrangements over a period of something like 25 years, during which there could be six or seven changes of government.

Even with deregulation of new tenancies, the high rent levels needed would mean that there would be 'little incentive for landlords to provide adequate accommodation except at the upper end of the market'. At such levels, most potential tenants would be better off buying and most would therefore do so. There are problems at the lower end of the market as well. The housing benefit regulations will not support rents judged to be too high, and the rents of many lower income families will not therefore be covered adequately enough to allow them to meet the new rents of the private sector. Doubts about whether the proposed deregulation will work have been expressed by the body which represents landlords, the British Property Association.[5]

Though some new privately-rented properties are likely to be produced by the removal of rent controls, the main boost to private renting seems likely to come from government-encouraged transfers out of council housing. The result will be an increase in private and housing association renting at the expense of council renting, rather than an increase in the total numbers of rented dwellings on the market.

The two proposed mechanisms for switching out of council housing are Tenants' Choice and Housing Action Trusts. It is not yet clear on what terms tenants will transfer out of council housing. In order to make the change attractive to tenants, the government will presumably have to ensure that rents stay at much the same levels as they were or would have risen to under council ownership or, if they rise, that there are commensurate benefits. But to make such a scheme work, the terms on which the new landlords acquired the property will have to be very generous to them, and there might be a public outcry against using public resources to subsidise private profits. Alternatively, or in addition, landlords who take over ex-council housing may 'asset strip' - sell homes off to owner-occupiers as they fall vacant, and this would gradually reduce the total stock available for renting.

The proposed Housing Action Trusts, after having improved their ex-council housing, will sell it to private landlords, housing associations or other bodies, with the option, if tenants prefer, of returning it to the local authorities. Again the terms under which property will be transferred to private landlords are not yet clear, but there seem to be the same difficulties as with Tenants' Choice.

It seems, to sum up, that the government's proposals are unlikely to have a very marked effect on the scale of private renting. More rented housing is certainly needed, as we have shown earlier. For reasons of history it is extremely unlikely that, whatever the government does, the private sector will be able to do anything substantial to meet the need. It seems unlikely that the changes in the 1988 Budget, intended to encourage investment in private renting, will make much difference. It follows that most of the necessary increase in rented housing will have to be in the form of social housing.

Forms of social housing

Social housing in one form or another will, therefore, not only remain the largest rental sector for as far ahead as anyone can see, but will also have to expand its stock if the need for rented housing is to be met.

The structure of the social housing sector in Britain cannot, however, remain as it is. For one thing the government itself is clearly determined to bring about change. The transfers out of council housing (through Tenants' Choice and Housing Action Trusts), the absence of new council building for rent and the proposed new financial regime for housing associations will alter the balance within the sector. The councils' share will fall; that of housing associations, cooperatives and other non-profit bodies will rise.

A readiness to move in this general direction is by no means confined to government circles. There is now widespread support for the view that many local authority housing empires are too large and too remote from their tenants, and that council administrations tend to be bureaucratic and inefficient. The need to weaken the current domination of social housing by council housing is now accepted by all the major political parties.

Some doubts have, however, been expressed about the wisdom of the policy, particularly if pushed too fast and too far. The first question is how far the current reputation of councils as landlords is justified in reality. Local authorities have faced extraordinarily difficult problems in recent years, first in trying to deal with the consequences of postwar mass housing and inner city decline, and later because of the financial constraints imposed by the government.

The Audit Commission, noting that the quality of management varied widely between councils, also pointed out that those with what they regarded as the worst performance were commonly those with the most difficult tasks:

> Some authorities have managed the situation better than others; and many of the Shire districts in particular do not suffer so much from the design mistakes and non-traditional building methods promoted by central government in the 1960s.

The government White Paper itself said 'In some areas the (council) system has provided good quality housing and management'.

Some experts argue that, although of course certain councils do not manage their housing as well as they might, the available evidence shows their general standards to be as high or higher than are found among the alternatives. The Institute of Housing, reviewing analyses of vacant properties, rent arrears and housing conditions, concluded that

'Taken as a whole council housing is managed at least as, and probably more, efficiently than other sectors of housing'.[6]

Another argument against demolishing council empires is that changes in the right direction are already taking place inside them. Many councils are trying to come to grips with the problems of bureaucracy and remoteness; they are decentralising housing management, promoting tenant participation and generally seeking to be more responsive to tenants as consumers. Such trends are being encouraged by the government's own Estate Action programme and its Priority Estates Project, which emphasise the advantages of local management and tenant involvement. This suggests that, if the current trends were given further support, there would be less need - some would say, no need - to look to alternative landlords.

A related point is about whether housing associations, cooperatives or other bodies (including, for that matter, private landlords) would be likely to do any better than councils. There is certainly no firm evidence that they would. The Institute of Housing concluded that 'transferring ownership or control of most of the public sector stock to bodies other than local authorities... will do nothing, of itself, to improve the quality of management'.

Such arguments do not constitute a convincing case for leaving the overwhelming bulk of social housing, as now, in the hands of local authorities. But they do suggest that it would be wise to move cautiously. It is noticeable that in the White Paper the government itself went back on some of the more sweeping changes it had aired earlier; it now proposes that 'Provision of housing by local authorities should *gradually* be diminished'.

Some other implications of the proposed switch also need to be explored. One anxiety is about rent levels, particularly in the light of the government's proposals to deregulate new housing association lettings, reduce government financial support to associations and attract more private finance and involvement into their operations. If as a result of these measures the rents in some housing association properties were much higher than in council housing, there would be two related consequences: low income families would be effectively excluded, and a new form of polarisation would develop between council housing and the new social housing agencies.

This kind of objection goes to the heart of one of the dilemmas about diversity in social housing. Diversity implies, not uniformity, but that agencies can within reason determine their own policies and sometimes set standards higher than others have adopted. Some social housing estates will be in more attractive locations, will be built to higher standards, will charge higher rents and will cater for better-off tenants. Some even will aim specifically for professional people, as do some of the French HLMs.

Furthermore, competition between different agencies ought to be welcomed; each should be seeking to make its housing the best quality (at least within a particular price range), the best value for money, the most attractive, the most efficiently managed. On these two grounds there can be no objection if some agencies have high rent policies, or even are more concerned than others with maintaining financial surpluses. And if social housing does contain this range of variations it will, arguably, help to improve the reputation of the sector as a whole.

The danger remains, however, that very different standards and much higher rents in some parts of social housing may encourage polarisation within the sector and radically alter its structure. The solution must lie in the balance that is struck, in any particular locality and nationally, between such 'up market' social housing bodies and the others. The more expensive housing should not dominate the local or national scene. There needs to be a framework, set by the government, within which the various types of social housing bodies are equitably treated and are given incentives to compete in providing a good service. Within that framework, it should be a responsibility of local authorities to keep a watching brief on agencies in their area and have the powers to ensure that the proportions of different kinds of social housing are reasonable to meet the district's needs, stepping in as necessary to encourage or directly promote new schemes. They could be helped in this, and in other tasks, by an official but independent Housing Inspectorate with a role something like that of the inspectorates which already exist for education and social services.

Since this is our first mention of this idea, we need to degress briefly to explain what we see as the Inspectorate's role. While being a public body, it should be genuinely independent. It would have positive functions as well as 'policing' ones. It would need to be established in the context of a government policy which was committed to continuing support for social housing. The existence of such an inspectorate would make it easier for both central government and local authorities themselves to play less of a day to day part in housing.

Another concern about the move towards pluralistic social housing is over the influence that tenants might have on the selection of newcomers. A common element in most of the proposals for the future is to give them more say in matters affecting their estates, and perhaps a part in the allocation of tenancies. This applies especially with proposals to increase the number of tenant cooperatives. There is clearly a strong case for tenants having more opportunity than most have at present to express their views. In particular, if their having a voice in allocation meant giving more consideration than councils currently do to the wishes of relatives and friends to live near each other - often with consequential benefits in informal care and support - it would be welcome. But some forms of tenant control could have deleterious results.

One danger is that giving tenants control over allocation could lead to the exclusion of what many of them might see as undesirable minorities - blacks, single parent families, unemployed people, people with mental handicaps. The effect of this would be to strengthen, rather than weaken, polarisation between estates, something which, as we have shown, is already encouraged by councils' own procedures. Council housing, and some council estates in particular, could on this score, as well perhaps as on others, come to be even more firmly established as the 'residual' part of the social housing sector. To avoid tenant control working in these ways, formal limits would need to be set. Encouraging agencies and their tenants to take the necessary broader view of their operations might be another task for local authorities, again backed by a Housing Inspectorate.

Like the more substantial qualifications mentioned earlier, these various points show that the process of changing the balance in social housing is more complex than the government seems to recognise. Nevertheless, the move towards pluralism in social housing deserves to be endorsed, as well as being to some extent inevitable. The dislike of large slow-moving bureaucracies, the distrust of local monopolies in social housing and the view that, as council decentralisation measures themselves suggest, local management and tenant involvement at the estate level are better than remote administrations - all these support the case.

Our own preference, within the new diversity in social housing, is for arms-length public bodies. Housing would be moved out of the local authority bureaucratic/political machine into new forms of housing agency in which the council would retain a controlling interest, perhaps shared with tenants or with other local bodies. Such arrangements would reduce bureaucracy, but contain an element of influence over policy on the part of locally-elected representatives. Subject to tenants' wishes, councils might be encouraged - or, if such schemes went well initially, obliged - to hive off all or part of their stock to a number of agencies which would act as trading bodies and be free of day to day local authority control and of departmentalism. Such new agencies would have some affinity to the OPAC version of *office public* HLMs mentioned in the previous chapter. As we have suggested, the OPACs themselves, with a broader base than local authorities but containing representatives of the local council as well as of other local participating bodies (such as the Chamber of Commerce) and of tenants, could themselves provide a direct model. It could be attractive in Britain, as it is in France, precisely because it balances autonomy and flexibility on the one hand and accountability to the various public and social interests on the other.

Whatever social housing forms are developed, it will be important to ensure that the fears we have expressed do not materialise, that differences between different social housing agencies do not lead to discrimination and further polarisation, and do not weaken the arrangements for mobility within the sector as a whole. To avoid excessive buraucracy or detailed intervention by local authorities, their roles and responsibilities - and the limits to these - would have to be carefully defined. In particular there would need to be a framework within which councils and other local social housing would work cooperatively. This could be yet another task for the proposed Housing Inspectorate. The important thing is to strike the right balance between autonomy and the broader public interest.

Above all, our discussion shows how unwise it would be for the government to rush precipitately into change on ideological grounds, as the 'gradualist' language of the White Paper suggests it may now have recognised. Public housing must have a continuing role of some importance as a landlord for a long time, over the next decade at least. How large its eventual role should be - how much of social housing should end up as council, how much in other forms - is something that can be decided over time, as the new styles of agency develop, increase their shares, demonstrate how effectively they can work and in particular how far they can steer clear of the dangers we have mentioned.

A comprehensive housing service
Though local authorities are likely to play a different and smaller role as landlords in the future, it is clear that they should assume some new responsibilities. This is recognised by the government in the White Paper, but we have identified some new tasks. In a strategic and surveillance role rather like that which local social services departments are increasingly expected to undertake for social care, local housing authorities would need to keep in touch with the other social and private landlords in their area and work to ensure an adequate supply of - and proper balance in - rented housing; to avoid forms of local control which led to further polarisation; and to contribute to effective national and local mobility schemes. They would need to be given new statutory responsiblities and powers.

Councils will perform such functions more effectively if they have some stake of their own in the local housing stock than if they have none. The experience of the Greater London Council in its later years shows that strategic housing authorities carry little weight if they do not have some housing involvement in their own right. They should have the power to invest in housing, through new building or by buying existing properties. But they would not necessarily act as direct landlords; they could, as we have suggested earlier, operate through arms-length subsidiaries, including bodies such as OPAC HLMs.

The suggestion of giving councils wider housing responsibilities is not a novel one. As long ago as 1968 the Seebohm Report argued that local authorities needed to 'know more about the total housing situation in their areas and the trends and developments that bear on it' and that they should 'become actively involved in the housing problems of their area'[7] and in 1978 the Housing Services Advisory Group devoted a report to the proposal that local authorities should take on this broader role.[8] The idea might have been successfully developed had it not been for the growing financial stringency and the continuing pressure on local authority finances.

The proposed increase in social housing by bodies other than themselves obviously strengthens the argument for local housing authorities taking on broader responsibilities. As the government itself recognises, only local authorities can take a comprehensive and long term view of housing needs in their districts. They should be given a statutory duty not only to assess needs but also to ensure that those needs are met through a variety of tenure arrangements, private and social. Their functions should include acting as developers of housing for sale to individual owners, and encouraging investment. They would set the climate, sometimes investing alone or in collaboration with others, and sometimes directly influencing investment through their land and planning powers. All this should be set in the context of a five-year local housing plan, rolling forward and subject to review each year. This proposed system would have much in common with the original conception, now largely abandoned, of local housing strategies and housing investment plans.

As part of ensuring that the stock in their area is maintained, local authorities should provide support to existing and potential owner-occupiers. The spread of home ownership has created large numbers of marginal owners, people whose incomes are barely adequate to sustain them as property owners. For such people, and for the many others in only slightly better circumstances, finance needs to be available to enable them to repair and maintain their homes. Finance is not the only problem. Home ownership puts people into positions of responsibility for important decisions about the management of maintenance, requiring investments of resources such as time, knowledge, stamina and confidence, all or any of which they may lack. As part of their comprehensive service, councils should be obliged to ensure that the necessary advice, information and help are available. To some extent these are already provided by the housing aid and advice centres run by some local councils. But the range of service needs to be expanded and to be offered in all areas, if not by the council itself then by another agency acting on its behalf.

Reforming housing finance

These various changes would do something to bring about a social housing sector better suited to the future than the present structure. But alone they are not enough to reverse polarisation and resolve the other current problems. Putting things right depends on repairing and improving the council stock and also on building more social housing in total. Neither of these can be done without more money. The government will need to provide additional direct resources or rents will have to rise, with the impact on poorer families being met through greater support with their housing costs. As we argued in the previous chapter in discussing the HLMs' problems over rents and benefits, rents cannot be raised without an adequate system of financial support. Hence the dilemma, in Britain as in France: how can the problems of social housing be tackled without increasing public spending, either on subsidies or on housing benefits? The answer is that they cannot.

The root of the current problem is the polarisation of financial treatment between owner-occupation and renting. This has developed over several decades but has become progressively more marked since the late 1970s. Tax relief on mortgages has increased dramatically, while support for council housing has been drastically cut. Between 1978-79 and 1986-87 the cost of mortgage relief in the United Kingdom doubled in real terms to about £4.5 billion. The bill has been rising steeply as more and more people have started to buy their homes and as house prices have risen faster than other prices.

We estimate on the basis of the government's public expenditure figures that, taking into account capital gains tax exemption, discounts on council house sales and mortage relief, the annual government subsidy to home ownership was over £9 billion in 1987-88. This compares with a total of about £4 billion, including housing benefit, going by way of subsidy to council tenants.[9]

Apart from the inequity, the present arrangements have other grave disadvantages. They fuel the process of polarisation between sectors. They encourage relatively well-off home owners to aquire more housing than they need or would otherwise buy. They push up house prices. They lead to a degree of labour immobility which is notoriously high in comparison with other advanced economies, and which puts a brake on the nation's economic growth.

These flaws have been widely recognised since at least 1985. In that year a consensus began to emerge among those outside the present government who had studied the subject. They included the Royal Institution of Chartered Surveyors,[10] the Archbishop of Canterbury's Commission on Urban Priority Areas[11] and the Duke of Edinburgh's Inquiry into British Housing.[12]

With such a strong body of authoritative opinion arguing for a fundamental change, the intellectual case for retaining the present system is in tatters. As the Duke of Edinburgh's Inquiry pointed out (and as its composition showed) this is not a party-political matter. The consensus is broad and is gathering momentum. The government's proposed replacement of a property tax (local rates) by the Community Charge or poll tax - which will be more regressive than rates in its impact - makes the case for reform even stronger.

The political difficulties are obvious. The government is committed both to restraint in public expenditure and to the maintenance of mortgage relief. But the system must be changed for something more just and more effective. The aims of a new scheme should be to treat poor people fairly as against better-off people, to avoid distorting housing markets and to ensure greater equity of treatment between owner-occupation and renting. Any new scheme would have to be affordable, administratively feasible and politically acceptable. It would have to be capable of being introduced gradually, so as to avoid unreasonably upsetting the domestic budgets of people who had entered commitments on the assumption that the present arrangements would continue.

A number of schemes have been suggested, some in more detail than others. The Royal Institution of Chartered Surveyors proposed a new financial structure, phasing out mortgage tax relief and substituting a new form of housing allowance available to all tenures.[13] Two PSI researchers outlined a reform of housing benefits, retaining mortage relief but reintroducing Schedule A income tax on the imputed rental value of owner-occupied homes.[14] The Duke of Edinburgh's Inquiry, calling for 'a more even-handed treatment' between owning and renting and a gradual shift to 'fiscal neutrality', advocated a 'need-related housing allowance' to replace mortgage tax relief and housing benefit. The Association of Metropolitan Authorities (AMA) suggested a two-tier system of support, with a flat-rate 'universal housing allowance' for owners and tenants alike, supplemented by a means-tested housing benefit.[15] An alternative solution would be to retain - and reform - mortgage tax relief, to extend similar relief to tenants and to complement this with a means-tested housing benefit for the remaining minority on the lowest incomes.

Each of these proposals has some disadvantages along with its attractions. Some would achieve the objectives more successfully than others. Any of them would be preferable to the current arrangements.

Whatever is done, some immediate - and complementary - changes are needed to give councils more financial elbow-room in handling their own housing finances. Local authorities should be free to spend what they receive from council house sales on improvement, aquisition or new building. This would of course mean that the government would have to allow an increase in the total level of capital spending on housing and relax the borrowing limits it at present imposes on the local authorities.

A major constraint on public housing investment in recent years has been the Treasury's insistence that money borrowed for capital projects counts towards the public sector borrowing requirement (PSBR). According to this view, borrowing by a private developer to build houses is somehow different in its impact on the economy from borrowing by a local authority for the same purpose. Such a view, based on accounting conventions rather than economic reality, is manifestly absurd. Public sector capital spending on housing should be excluded from the PSBR.

Direct policies on polarisation

The proposed extension and upgrading of social renting, based on a new financial structure, would in the longer term have the effect of reducing polarisation between tenures. But we need to consider other policies to tackle polarisation directly, both in the meantime and in the long term.

Polarisation between council and owner-occupied housing can be somewhat lessened by reducing spatial concentration. The less that particular geographical areas are seen as 'council', and therefore inferior, the less that tenants will suffer as a result of stigma, stereotyping, 'ghettoisation' and low morale.

This consideration throws a different light on council house sales. There is no doubt about the drawbacks of the Right to Buy policy. It weakens council housing because it disposes of the best of the council stock, and leaves less rented housing available for those who need it. But at the same time it has created more of a mixture of owners and tenants on certain estates. So in some places the policy has had positive consequences, on top of its obvious benefit in opening owner-occupation to some people who would otherwise be unable to enter the market.

In any event, the Right to Buy policy is here to stay, whatever the political complexion of the next government. It will continue to be easier for councils to sell houses on suburban estates than flats in inner city blocks, but every effort should be made to promote tenure mix in the less popular estates. This cannot be done by providing financial incentives to sitting tenants to buy unpopular flats - by trying to sell the unsaleable. It depends on sizeable investment in such estates to make them attractive enough for people - present tenants or those from outside - to want to buy homes there. Tenure mix will be easier when people wish to live on such estates. This raises a general point about how to deal with the unpopular estates.

A strategy of encouraging more spatial mixture among tenures would need to have two other elements. One would be for local authorities or other social housing landlords to acquire additional properties for renting through the open market. There are management objections to this kind of 'pepper-potting', but if it were done on a substantial enough scale it would again reduce the influence of tenure in itself. Second, and in the longer term, social housing bodies should, themselves or through mixed schemes of the kinds mentioned earlier, build mixed tenure estates in which new homes for sale are mingled with those for rent.

Measures like these would do little to reduce polarisation *within* social housing, unless accompanied by other actions to deal with the physical, management and social conditions on the worst estates. We have described the processes through which disadvantaged people find themselves living on such estates. They lack the bargaining power which would enable them to exercise the choices open to others. Of course, hardly anybody has an entirely free choice over their housing; what they end up with is constrained in all sorts of ways by what is available and by what they can afford. But it is surely worth asking why some tenants should be expected to live in estates where, given a free choice, virtually nobody would wish to live.

Such estates need to be so radically refurbished, by councils, housing associations, trusts, private landlords or developers, as to be transformed into places where some people would positively choose to make their home. Alternatively, where this would be inadequate or too costly, they should be demolished. A continuing assault on these lines would do more than anything else to ensure that the poorest people were no longer in the worst social housing, in addition to all its other benefits to residents. There are already enough examples on individual estates to what can be done by way of refurbishment. But the scope and scale are too small. The new Housing Action Trusts might be able to add something to the efforts of Estate Action and the Priority Estates Project. But the drive needed depends on adequate resources for investment in social housing; given the present distribution of government financial support for housing, these are unlikely to be forthcoming. Changes are needed if the worst current examples of social housing are to be eradicated or upgraded, and if polarisation is to be drastically reduced.

Conclusion

A picture may be emerging of the kind of social housing we have in mind for the future. We have shown that more rented housing is needed in Britain, and we have argued that the privately-rented sector is unlikely to achieve more than a modest contribution to the necessary increase. It follows that social housing will not only continue to be the largest rented sector but will also need to expand.

Such a role for social housing would depend on a positive government commitment, backed by adequate resources. The government would recognise the importance of the sector as a key element in the nation's housing system, as it is in France, and one which, as there, commanded all-party backing. Social housing would be a strong and healthy sector containing a range of good quality dwellings, owned and run by a plurality of agencies. Social housing would not be the Cinderella sector it is at present, but another option alongside home-ownership operating on more or less equal terms, and complemented by a small private rented sector. It would, as now, house relatively more poor people than other sectors - inevitably, because they would for the most part neither be current owners nor able to buy, and the rents of such private property as was available would usually be beyond their means.

But as well as meeting the needs of those who could not buy their homes, it would, alongside the smaller private rented sector, also provide rented housing for the various groups of people who for one reason or another preferred not to buy. They would include young single people, students, people moving to a new area for work or other reasons, young couples not yet sure whether or where they wanted to settle, and people who simply preferred to avoid the responsibility of maintaining their own home. There would be more such people in rented housing now if the financial advantages were not so heavily weighted in favour of owner-occupation. Some of them, as in some French HLMs, would be professional people, managers and the like.

As Harloe has argued, given such a policy - with genuine choice and attractive alternatives to home ownership - 'it might become the norm for a substantial proportion of the population to move easily between the two main sectors during their lifetime as and when their circumstances demanded either rented or owner-occupied housing'.[16] The fact that as many as a fifth of those on current council waiting lists are owner-occupiers, mainly elderly people, shows that the demand already exists, though at present it cannot be met.

We have suggested some of the actions needed to move from where we now are to a future of this kind, and we have tried to draw on the experience of France in doing so. The comparative element of the review shows that there are some differences in the organisation of social housing in France and Britain, but a high degree of similarity in their problems and some similarities but also some variations in recent policy responses by the respective governments.

The main conclusion from the cross-national comparison is that in both countries the problems result not from particular procedures or institutional structures but from more fundamental trends, fuelled by government policies which, in both countries, are inequitable in their treatment of renting as against owning. The French, in other words, have made much the same basic policy mistakes as the British.

Nevertheless, it looks as if Britain could usefully draw upon French experience in some respects. One example is the National Commission's programme of estate improvement, on a proportionately larger scale and with a broader social perspective than our own. Secondly, in seeking diversity in social housing, the HLM model has something to offer, and in particular the OPAC form. As we have pointed out, this arrangement, combining a large degree of independence with ultimate accountability to a board representing public bodies and tenants, has something in common with the arms-length local authority-based agencies we ourselves propose.

Such changes, though helpful, would not however achieve very much by themselves. Most of the current debate about policy gives inadequate attention to the impact on social housing of the long term shifts between tenures, of social and demographic changes, of the economic recession, or of the ways in which the consequences of all this are - and have been since before 1979 - reinforced by official policies. The effects are already being felt in owner-occupied housing also, where there are growing problems of repair and maintenance and of mortgage defaults. A radically new set of policies is needed. The political difficulties are acknowledged. But the reform of housing finance has now become urgent. Change is needed so that Britain can have not only better social housing but also a wider choice of homes for everybody.

References

(1) Secretaries of State for the Environment and Wales, *Housing: the Government's Proposals,* Cm 214, London, HMSO., 1987.

(2) G. Bramley and D. Paice, *Housing Needs in Non-Metropolitan Areas,* Report of research carried out for the Association of District Councils, Bristol, University of Bristol, School for Advanced Urban Studies, 1987.

(3) Audit Commission, *Managing the Crisis in Council Housing,* London, HMSO, 1986.

(4) C.M.E. Whitehead and M.P Kleinman, *Private Rented Housing in the 1980s and 1990s,* Cambridge, Granta Editions for the University of Cambridge Department of Land Economy, 1986.

(5) *The Times,* 20 October 1987.

(6) Institute of Housing, *Preparing for Change. Public Sector Housing: Future Use, Control and Management,* A Report Prepared by a Working Party of the Institute of Housing, London, Institute of Housing, 1987.

(7) Seebohm Report, *Report of the Committee on Local Authority and Allied Personal Social Services,* Cmnd 3703, London, HMSO, 1968.

(8) Housing Services Advisory Group, *Organising a Comprehensive Advisory Service,* London, Department of the Environment, 1978.

(9) Her Majesty's Treasury, *The Government' Public Expenditure Plans 1988-89 to 1990-91,* Cm 288, I and II, London, HMSO, 1988.

(10) Royal Institution of Chartered Surveyors, *Better Housing for Britain,* London, Royal Institution of Chartered Surveyors, 1985.

(11) Archbishop of Canterbury's Commisssion on Urban Priority Areas, *Faith in the City,* London, Church House Publishing, 1985.

(12) Duke of Edinburgh's Inquiry, *Inquiry into British Housing: Report,* London, National Federation of Housing Associations, 1985.

(13) Royal Institution of Chartered Surveyors, op. cit.

(14) R. Berthoud and J.Ermisch, *Reshaping Benefits: the Political Arithmetic,* London, Policy Studies Institute, 1985.

(15) Association of Metropolitan Authorities, *A New Deal for Home Owners and Tenants: a Proposal for a Housing Allowance Scheme,* London, AMA, 1987.

(16) M. Harloe, 'The Green Paper on housing policy', in M. Brown and S. Baldwin (editors), *Year Book of Social Policy in Britain*, London, Routledge and Kegan Paul, 1978.